# COLLECTED POEMS

**Ian Patterson** taught English for almost twenty years at Queens' College, Cambridge, where he is now a Life Fellow. His academic writing includes *Guernica and Total War* (Profile, 2007) and numerous essays on twentieth-century writers; his translations include Fourier, *The Theory of the Four Movements* (Cambridge University Press, 1996) and Proust, *Finding Time Again* (Penguin, 2004). He has published over a dozen works of poetry, including *Time to Get Here: Selected Poems 1969-2002* (Salt, 2003) and *Marsh Air* (Equipage, 2019). His poem 'The Plenty of Nothing' was awarded the Forward Prize for Best Single Poem in 2017. He lives in Suffolk.

# Collected Poems

Ian Patterson

Broken Sleep Books

## Editor's Note

Where poems have been published in more than one book, only the first publication of the poem has been included in this collection.



ISBN
Paperback: 978-1-915760-57-9 Hardback: 978-1-916938-95-3



Cover designed by Aaron Kent

Typeset by Aaron Kent

With thanks to Will Shutes

Broken Sleep Books
PO Box 102
Llandysul
SA44 9BG

# CONTENTS

A THING OF REASON 11
Pencil, Fatal Congeries, As We Run Out of the Wet, Man, Bound to a Time, Japan is Sad, Sentinel, Requiem for a Brain, Notes

ENDLESS DEMANDS 23
Things Reply, Uncle Apprehension, Why Motoring Costs Have Soared, Holding on to a Stranger (with Nick Totton), Tatlin's Dream, Hardly Yippee, We Must Tighten Our Belts, Metaphorically, The light determines a state of absolute rest?, Out of Date, It Was a Long Lane, I Felt a Hand Grip My Elbow, Endless Demands, The Chronicler

NO DICE 47
So to Speak, After Breakfast

ROUGHLY SPEAKING 53
All Our Ends, Still life, Without Rhyme or Reason, It Had to be You, The Origins of Love and Hate, Late Capital, Irreducible Blue, Speaking of Life, Prattle, You Never Said, Red Priest, Interference, Matter and Memory, Apropos, II, Time How Short, Far and Away, No Resolution, The Night The, Postcards to Spain 1986, Postcard to Italy, A Reading, L'Histoire, Small Changes, Guinea on China, High Time, The First Intervention, When It Seemed That All Was Lost, Solo, Wherever a Head, The Name of Day, Say Nothing

TENSE FODDER 97
A Bit Apart, Look Back, Lino Cut, The Garden Party, Sleep, This and That, No Contact, These Days, The Wire, Less and Less, Facing Page, Drying Out

MUCH MORE PRONOUNCED 123
Some Title, Much More Pronounced

from TIME TO GET HERE 143
Poem, The Elegy for Spring, Kara Chach, Quiet Arriving, Summing It Up One of These Days, A Happy New Year, Waking Up: 2.10 PM, Politics, Night Ministry, Lullaby, Ritual Slips, Polly Fortune, Red Breath, Hold the Child Father Sunlight, Sparkling Fruit Salts, The Yurt: Day One, The Audience, Life Dreamed is Now Life Lived (David Gascoyne), Derry, The Political Economy of Art. Underground, Looking at Henry, Sestina, New

York, Oh Snooty, Oh, To Be in England, Pastoral, After Pope, Laugh Like a Piano, Basic White, Hardihood, Quite Right, A World of Love, Death of Dance, In the Train, North, Living Here Now, Mulch Tumult

THE GLASS BELL 211
Glossalgia, Glossolalia, Glossoplegia, P.S.

TIME DUST 235
Title Disputed, How Things Are, Wood, No Tongue, Not Quite Time, Still Visible, Last Year's Light, Simply That, This Umber Sea About Us, Avian, A Film, Deep, Easy to Say, Red, Fire, Corncrakes, Drawn Shapes, Trace, Crumpled, Light Paper Material

STILL LIFE 267
No Way, Warning Ignored, The Mode That Will Not Be Written, Seedy Box, Night View, One, Image Damage, Brown Paper, Footsteps, Empty Space, Cold Again, Rebuke

SPARE RIMES 283
The Field, Of Art, Paradise Lost, Saturday, Loud Bees, Where's the Fun?, Protected Wood, Not an Object, Hung Out, A Quieter Light, Small Change, Just Ignore Them

BOUND TO BE 299
Plenty of Nothing, Sunk in the Night, An Ear To Cry On, Northern Line, Old Details, Will Do, True Rendition, A Bit Part, Free Amble, By the Banks of Grim Margin, Crossing, Limbo, The Works, Saving Time, Could Be, The Scar, The Progress

MARSH AIR 333

TO ACCOUNT FOR 353
About the Dark, Look at Them, Consolidated Uproar, Inlaid Reflection, Just Thermal Slash, Faint Last Abandon, Intuition Rush, Allowance to Hand, Coppice Fret Verge, Overt Ruffle Return

SHELL VESTIGE DISPUTED 365
Orpheus Says, Something in the Air, Nothing Doing, Peculiar Pertinence, Planted Presence, Implacable Grasp, Nearly Stopped, Lapsed Step, More Measure, Least Ground, Flagrant Number, Least Ignorance, Clear Nothing, Tight Orbits, Provoke Better, Defeated Scale, Dark Otherwise, Doubtless Matter, Strong Original, Bedevilled Terms, Actual Selection,

Whirled Attention, Impression Really, Peep Contact, Earlier Pocket, Sense According, Air Flitter, Gloomy Clamber, Exceed Frame Time, Get an Ear Test, Potentially Permanent, Please Call Us, Why Call it Again?, Only Displacement, Past Taste, Leaving No Trace, Of Denser Things, A Hasty Dip, What Ever Next?, Another Subject Incline, Infernal Duo, Radish Nostalgia, Lemon Sole, I'm Not Sure, All Mere Use, Wilding Paper, Imported Raw

UNCOLLECTED POEMS 425

Some Constants, Herman, what makes you tick?, pourquoi chercher le bout de la chaîne qui nous relie à la chaîne?, Happy Endings, Ideal Fingers, 60 Windows, For John James, Poem for Numbers, Iron Letters, Coda, Wyatt's Voices

## COLLABORATIONS

MORE FOLLOWS 467

More Follows, Syringe Song, Big Boys Don't Fly, Taking the Stitches Out, Remember Dorking and Damn Malthus, Steam Radio, A Little Stranger, There Is No Parliamentary Road to Happiness, A Little Too Much Salt, A Separate Section on Hegel, A New Kind of Washing Machine, A Disturbance on the Acropolis

LOVE LAUGHS AT LOCKSMITHS 485

Behind the line the life lies, Making a statement fit, For Denise Riley, Men! Write Now, Wheat Stone Bridge, An arrow pointing to the top right hand corner, Out! Out! Out!, Just a friendly warning, Martin Webster sucks Paul Foot is a fairy, Strange to think he'll soon be sixty, The best thing is that it speaks about the future, the worst thing is that it speaks about the past, Suitable for thinking at any time, Morphologies, Love laughs at locksmiths, Special offer

INDEX OF POEM TITLES 505

# A THING OF REASON

*Black Suede Boot Press*, 1974

## *Pencil*

At the back of the building sacks empty
lemon fills my eyes with tears; such is
the music of restoration in your hands
spread like teeth before a blind composer.
Faultless drizzle from the fountain cuts
arches about you: anxiety hangs in it
ripe for my bunches of fingers; alert
it pulls the white stick, the fox is afraid,
low cloud obscures your last envelope. Carry
what you can, outline your eyes with poppyseed
as you leave me. I'll wait in the kitchen.
Sweet houseflies will predict the dissolution
of an order from this heap of patois: only
outside a pencil stalks the implacable day.

## *Fatal Congeries*

A lost view ungums my lips, matches
this coat of painted wood, horns are sprout-
ing, this head of mine sings uncontrollably
of woodland sawbenches & the figure of my
grandfather. Eagle feathers lie about under
the table picturing a weak climax to a
long chain of feathered betrayal; as I sleep
I lose all my visions into a pot of
goose and celery stew. Go on, march as you
smoulder, it's the smell of your boots I
love through all the century's smells. If
a thousand neckscarves are waved on a day like
this, the earth shudders and arms itself
for entire bodies to walk into the consequence.

# *As We Run Out of the Wet*

You," she said. I'm cast as matter, an over-
mirror of your waving barley
long meeting between the teeth
what did my fingers, a man
Also I eat wild things, what did
Book showing a single logic.    I
it sat quietly and ate my brain

# *Man*

A tremendous glitter widens my opinion of
the war beyond her thin grey face and my yellow
fingers. I am cheese; this plateau offers me
as a yellow cube. I refuse the darkness
and the sinuous attempts of promise in my
imagination half-governed and waving beside the
river like a nest of curly black hair that turns
to rain and pits me. I fall apart and
trickle down my forehead like a star
I hear the grass at my knees coming.
Whatever has been eating the fern lies on canvas
and dreams of the stepping sheep; I put out
my hand from the trestle table and touching
its wool I am content to watch the town blown up.

## *Bound to a Time*

Hope burns his hand on this concourse
listening for the law we round up and
eat off, those eyes a pitiful month
on my wall, a collar loose and white.
Wanting to go you raise your fist de-
riving the new grammar in a grand we; and
walk out pushing our bonhomie where the wet
men listen after years of hunger. All
afternoon I thought this was a delegation
of short words for struggle. Lunarcharsky
rises like the sun out of his overcoat;
the law, the cusps furnished reconstitution,
settle to the class of all things, his
hand raised where the bird flies, his face.

# *Japan is Sad*

I put my eyes in trust whose inflected words
twitch on the table between us. They flicker, I am
not going to blow up the sheep, emblem of my
mortal love. Wear my clothes and it'll rain.
The unfortunate traveller whose feet I point
at the road is dead. Weep for him. Conform his
shape to your hands' air and ventilate his
sad hope as the fire is fanned with lexical beauty.
        It is the only sponge I have, this platform
and my breath makes it sway as it washes my features from
the code. What kind of mirror is it absorbs
light when my flames can be seen for miles? When
the sun rose advertising the moon in the words
of history, who turned from the east and smiled?

## *Sentinel*

Would a house by the lake, a small grammar of
silent looks win the struggle he wondered. A mythology
of faces can satisfy a need for clarity without
the burden of association we have known. Ears and tongues
mark out time as the women come and go, whose only
dream is the end of the world they invent as the laws
we leave behind whenever we spread our fingers to an
innocent flame burning in our eyes. Write the invention
of truth in your capable suggestions. They wave
like a vision
            and leave me fixed and not decaying
not a snapshot. Radical clauses exact no tribute
from the street; a day like this enfolds the inside
real moment in a clasp of inextinguishable sentiment.

## *Requiem for a Brain*

Plunge your heart. The scarved
figures step out of hearing
to demand my reprieve. I will be
scanned and made to balance where
soaring hope fell between my teeth
and my breathless jaw. Oh let me
sing in nervous light, give me the
clay of skulls to work in free
afternoons. Will is nothing but
a thing of reason.

## *Notes*

Will is nothing but a thing of reason.
There are different ways of perceiving the world.
Nations are bound by the limits of a language.
Nobody but a nice girl loves a sailor.

# ENDLESS DEMANDS

*Holophrase*, 1983

## *Intro*

After how
this wound
close when
I was thought
on my knee
is history. The
history of
my memory
is not
in the corner
of my
change in this.

## *Talkin' Bout Things*

congealed air at the windows in June making
all our time burst like sweat behind my shoulders

a million grass seeds water the garden
in a hose of dust, a display of bleeding

breathless and gritty politics of the photographic present
Books flower and fade and I forget them. It was 96 degrees

It was not true although we call it sleep. Attractive bulb
rash Shelleyan flutter, tie the windows with string

le monde rentre dans un sac. You said you had to go to sleep
and did it, falling to type up your life on a sample pillow

Garden herb more nameless than a vision of it
by what it leaves out, hung and dried for the jar

We sidle about, keeping our minds on money, broadcast
utter failure of purchased hope. They lost it all.

Brief on the hoof it was, legs crossed by the stair against peeling
blue. Our hot child breathes. The myths in the air make me tired.

## *Things Reply*

If I close one eye
I remember migration
into fiery trees

feet straight at him
little sparrows and a starling
no pigeons

lazy ideas
tremble on your breath
like beads of water

slivers of yellow
language which
teaches itself

I am overcome
and go home to
white, grey, black.

## *Uncle Apprehension*

The grasping skeleton
divides rooms, wallpaper paste,
repeats until my eye is blunt
Are you there? Force. Axons pioneer
routes of time and sympathy,
capillary indecision
blurs the industrial delta.

What is the object of living here?

Arriving for the day shift
as it dawns the modern age
reappears in the words of this street
the object is an object for everybody
as it dawns, the single, public light.

## *Why Motoring Costs Have Soared*

Note also the amusing attempts of the author and adding
that this unity "money" is not something actual. Truth is
all-sided, of nature by man from moment to moment. What
is your favourite amount of cognition? Not yet developed,
not yet unfolded, perhaps a hint of vacillation here?
Under the heading "ices of every description" they kept
shop, into space and time at the hands of expert layout
technicians. Could be earning a hundred a week minimum
somewhere else. But you'll remember the glossy cigarette packet
too. Pull out the cigarettes *by means of* the gold tab
and offer them to all the persons present. *Proffer* your
lighter – it will save embarrassment. The universal is the
foundation, and burns clearly after dark.
Ignition? "The history of thought equals the history of
language??" (Lenin). Ah! The necessity of connection. The
international monetary fund and the traffic warden. A two
act play by Fernando Arrabal. Nobody can afford to see it.
I say nobody, (embarrassed cough), I assume your basic
acceptance of the "Immanent emergence of distinctions"
and the heavy germanic cast of your eyebrows. Do I
exclude the most germane, the gold glint on your wild wings?

# *Holding on to a Stranger*

*An ode to dialectical materialism, written with Nick Totton*

**I**

your hand flaccid on the steel pin of hope
a vision in the sky, over the falling
blue, empty day
whose purpose is a mystery to us

whoever is on the radio (like a
persistent fly, but immobile…
throw nothing away
whose purpose is a mystery

to us; it is a mistake which
there will be payment for
& it has gone where the roof sags
overdetermined by the day

come over here, don't try to interrupt the
squelchy biomorphic goings-on
it's the only way I know
whose purpose is a mystery

**2**

we fence in truth
danger in the sky posing for re-entry
inhibition mechanisms carve an arc
now it has gone.

where the roof sags
thought hit a new variant
constructing a visit from the air
the only way it knows

a flaccid hand on the steel pin
of hope, that holds a visionary city
in the sky-blue, empty day
whose purpose is the only mystery
I know

**3**

the city never proposed to star
in your collusions; come over here
and pose as a square meal,
it's the only way

I know the roof sags
like voices, always further away,
slipping by the fence, their embarrassed pain
a mystery to us

through the overdetermined blue day
which nobody listens to
a stranger's caress
touches the steel pin

don't try to listen, don't
try to interrupt
the blue empty day
whose only purpose is mystery

**4**

the fence in the sky is a true
square meal for the eye
which runs blindly along the steel pin
into the blue empty day

the only way I know
gathers the mistakes together,
and on the radio
the voices sound hopeful and further away

don't fail to listen
and look for the nature of things
the roof sags purporsefully
like a visit from the sky

from impersonal landscapes
beyond the sagging fence
of the mysterious, blue, empty day
that no-one can interrupt

**5**

come over here as a
kind of square meal for the eye
persistently overdetermined
by the blue, empty day

whose purpose is a butterfly
on the steel pin of hope
like a visit from impersonal land-
scapes of memory

don't fail to listen
and look at the nature of things
it's the only way I know
to turn on the radio

because you never proposed to star
in a movie of falling day
so we mustn't interrupt the blue, empty day
whose purpose is the only way we know

# *Tatlin's Dream*

light and colour when they slip off the only
source there is, too late for actual use
past the moment of realisation, as tears
ran down his smooth face, enough finance
to protect him as he sleeps in sorrow
and the weather operates gently with snow
and other quiet things. And time in barrels
horseshoe marks in the turf, mud
and broken collarbones of November in the
money. No prison, only pain when I move it
and I may receive visitors. He was there
too long, the leather decayed. No tiring insistence
that the significance you create is the result
of a mediating process, wispy symbols of nationalist
intrigue, just a sky singing in an empty sky
as we watched the race from the heather
no — cancel & insert 'Colour is dealt with in
the language of colour in these large paintings:
do not talk to me again.' I looked down on the
course; above me the sky was clear, the light hard;
my boots glistened with wet; some of the almost
white sand coated the toe of each boot. It was
chalky. I will not say what I could hear
noises obtrude and represent pain of course. You
won't get a word out of me until I have stayed too long.
This is a silent blackbird photographed leaving
the stock exchange, this is the end of an era.

## *Hardly Yippee*

over miles of flat land
blows the concrete dust

red and white things
in the forsaken windows

his long legs volunteering
that heart for the future

they never installed "correct breathing"
a lack which pleased the critics

huge clouds pass
like dungarees

in his hands was his head
in his head was his heart

along the minute rifling
were inscribed the words

"we now know that work should be
man's most beautiful occupation"

there is no such thing
as preparation for construction

## *We Must Tighten Our Belts*

cold blue mouth clenched
as determinate origin
no kidding

just having a long conversation
silence descends quicker
than we think

and placid the scissors lie
on the paper
I forgot to ask

difficulties on the inter-city
out of the backwoods
dense tufts of pine

distance hits the window
I am heaved
into the future

like the smug curve of mortgage interest
into the balance of the proud father
of a nation warming to his job

# *Metaphorically*

Contact at shops at bus stops at places where we
drink stars shining bright in the little sky and hum
of the dominant series in both ears no bees could lift
my head off like this music will not stop and getting louder
my field of vision shrinks and optic nerve strains
cannot deliver the goods they get too big for their boots
and while not laughing or growing any other way men and women
I don't know enlarge their hair-crowned heads to bend towards
me words and memory assaults. It will take the curious
strength of a moment of thought to recoil from the impending tone
and hate with effort and critical severity sentences
employed like us as advertisements as warnings now to appropriate
the sentences employed for ephemeral consumption of the central
personality, the tune of the market piped into a booming sound
of slippers on pavements as the sky glooms over and dour
afternoons clouds gather above the isle of dogs, approach of
more domination huge face of no response no traveller returns
unless the sale, we are proceed and grow our enormous soul chopped
into splinters who populate and are the concrete
potentials unhandled by the touch of vision behind her national
health spectacles oh minerva with the pointed frames on which no
star will rest until the day comes with the promise of no more of it.

## *The light determines a state of absolute rest?*

You need to have a transformation
        formula to relate this to that and language
                        shaken apart as a matter
of exchange
                rising at seven to the cupboard
                blade cooked up to prevent it.
This vice of thought
    was sweating for a tin-opener
            as I remember it
like a mould fringe on a picture in the townhall
or a size cut too small from the inside.
        They have trampled to the moon
                for a young delivery of news
                        on the open market
                and come back with
        lino cuts.
Fundamental uneasiness about this a state of mind, then,
    in time for it.

## *Out of Date*

Today an overt hunger for unity
sweeps between them and
returns to apply white thoughts
to the business of our next impulse
but lets it drop
        into a great vacuity
the crowd's idea of Australia
        or the disc of a sun bottle
everyone watches it fly over
like a second home
        balancing a bucket
                in a reflection of a ticket
        *at which point they realised that the solution*
                *of the "problem" involved*
                *a redefinition of the customary concept of time.*

## *It Was a Long Lane*

bricks beckon irreducibly
to heat up, colourless scream,
or condense our programme
for photographing pain
in a bridge to cognition interference —
a minute of psyonic cantilever
among thousands against hundreds
a more open gesture
dropping charges with sentiment
utter mess, pure food, organic prelude,
maxim overdraft on rehearsed information
and the rest of the lunchtime
entertainment team will stay away.

# *I Felt a Hand Grip My Elbow*

All right, the air is full of lies
and you breathe it, desire them
from the first
getting a measure of our sobbing
inelegance from the yellowed writings
of the permawar philosophers.
Our familiar phlegm lurks on the membrane
too smart to take up the struggle
from the soiled discs,
luminous faces in the tube
a swagger of cultural politics
in the cradle of tubular men
with no response to the rest
but quietly determined to unleash the silly hatchet
on its one-way journey to the burial ground
and harness the relentless pulp
to a word in someone's ear
to find out about you, I mean
you don't like it either, do you?

Then there was Vegetable Satire, a
lonely subject snarled on star-time
without money for a facelift
or a tool of thought
with studs on the inside
limit — it's all they had
until war entered the canopy of their wildest dreams
singing some Cole Porter number in
a storm like third-hand Shakespeare in a shopping bag.

Turn to the left, turn to the right,
turn to the stars as they
shine all night
like the bone in your teeth it' s
home for the beast in your bath.

***

And that distilled resentment
that satirical old erection
keeps the whole show on the road
year after year

## *Endless demands*

Oh, don't you start, it's
the discrete mode of address
full of numbers
steel noise at the edge
of a vertical band, the page
and the stolen letter
strict and remote
fluttering from the pointed lie.
The sky stops
with a lyrical fist-stagger
and your mouth is
already manufacturing a world.
Everyday demands
is a good deal to take
without an entirely extra coming war
without history
or music
or work on one alternative
after conceiving
the thought experiment.
But the chips are
down, the
word is out.

# *The Chronicler*

A replica city
glass meets eye and sees through it
hands rub over the pavement

curling into names
that control the city
basking in dry grass

cylindrical plane trees
in the jointed evening
men rule lines

surrounded by paper and metal
you might decide to discard the air
How unearthly!

or fall under that gaze
plate glass, leather, pink fingers
force to force as they scream

replica time
in the Greenwich web
body oscillating at some unlikely frequency

# NO DICE

*Poetical Histories*, 1988

## *So to Speak*

Heroes easily run aground on reasons
but they're insatiable among the relics
of flame and light
or else they look up and see what's in the air

Nature spars with the profit motive
until cool waters are dulled
and everybody's eyes look as dead as last year
with its echo mirroring the skies

Humans like us are eaten up with things
and every step we take
needs a little bit of blindness
or a man on the road to a port

As dispirited as surrealism
we may drop into a sort of reverie
where bells ring for no good reason
and voices emerge from faces

Some heroes love to hear
their chains rattling
inside them
on the way to meetings

Often they speak the language
but use thought as a whip
against the hands of time
so to speak

They also crumple things up
crush them inside and out
and then appear surprised
when they can't find the edge.

## *After Breakfast*

Somewhere else in the time spectrum
sweet morning drips from the line
white yogurt to ease my throat
I caught it on a nail I almost said
thorn although it was your eyes
that caught my breath and made me pause

Appeased by food I was attacked
by resentment and became something else wrong
with the world I was not born to get
it right I muttered through tense teeth
knowing that we should fight for what we love
not are, twenty years since Frank O'Hara died

In this world of intersecting manifolds
of power and circulation it is simply good
that afterimages that change or remain
in the night or day should keep flowing
and never be the same twice,
the flower's metamorphosis to the flood

I.e. the poem, which is the opposite
of an ark but sings at your gait
against the iridescent pages of modernism
descending a staircase or starting a car
forwards in the garage of the twentieth century
which looks unlikely but is the only way out

This is not literally true but I
have chosen all the statements freely
and do not a prison make even when hallucinations

hover round my heart and ears at night
or by day become coincidences of such beauty
I could weep at not believing in horoscopes.

# ROUGHLY SPEAKING

*Cambridge*, 1990

*One morning I walked back through the park, and saw the highest branches of a tree draped with bits of marabout, with some sort of silk, with two or three odd stockings and, wrapped round the top of the tree, like a cloak quick-thrown over the shoulder of some high-born hidalgo, some purple damask. Below it, balanced on a twig as if twirled round a finger, was a brand new bowler hat. They had all been blown across the road from a bombed hotel opposite. A surrealist painter whom I knew slightly was staring at this, too. He said: "Of course we were painting this sort of thing years ago, but it has taken some time to get here."*

— Inez Holden, *It Was Different at the Time*

*Dans un monde unifié on ne peut s'exiler. Qu'ai-je donc fait pendant ce temps?*

— Guy Debord, *Panégyrique*

## *All Our Ends*

There is something to be said
as the forms cough in the cold street

We need to know what it is
and we wait for a voice in the words

As we look at imperialism in the glass
hearing the wrong white words

The early crocuses listen in sudden frost
That wraps us in anticipation

The face on the screen looks back at me
And says "this is the being that started the necessary conflict

The world is also in him, and the words
Make space for it, if he struggles to listen

Absorbing and opening to it in the tide
Of everything he is. Are you ready?"

Discountenanced, the dead voice stops.
Corn dust and clutter fall lightly everywhere

Coating distrust and social engineering in a single thought
Of all our ends, so that it also fills our mouths.

## *Still life*

Reconsidering the track that parts the wind
as black thirst when there's nowhere else
but the necessary pain of women
ever to be found among other lines

when chanting like a leaf keeps you awake
and images at the defined by torn sounds
in a few stops in the pitch dark
the afternoon light the merest streaming memory

some earthly fear of foot on stones and eyes
and what if your hands are full of a stifled voice
like guilt night after night saying don't give up
crowds are rising inside me on the line

these were the days lost in guesswork
and careful production of the stars
the women I mentioned chiselled the material
and laminated all the time in the world

at that period the water was all painted grey
the swan and its white shadow was outside
as white as arctic silence with both eyes open
and snow teeth instead of lashes

## *Without Rhyme or Reason*

I may be without rhyme or reason
I may be watched by eyes of consequence
I may be the idea of the future shimmering like a summer holiday
I may be shrouded in a defiant haze
I may be driving from place to place
I may be pictures browning at the edges
I may be unjustifiably bad-tempered
I may be controlled by hidden strings or more likely not
I may be reflected expectantly in their unsubdued eyes
I may be turning over a new leaf
I may be on the night train or on the television news
I may be a conceptual possibility
I may be like they always did before
I may be walled in
I may be like multiple speech
I may happen very naturally
I may be looks that have lingered
but roughly speaking I cannot be unchanged

# *It Had to be You*

When you watch a Spanish movie, you can speak it
but you have to abandon everything.
What you imagine you empty of thought and lines of beauty
& what you do is joined to the dead hours.
          Grey light falling on naked angles.
I shall break on you, too. Day thumps with a heavy step.
What you (you) imagine is neither here nor there
and we are both in between it together.
          Now where? the view (of clean lake and damp earth)
might be a specifically male one,
with entwined postcards on a sable ground.
It will become too dark for words:
belly of sleep with its humble fingers in the butcher's tray.

What you do right is dissatisfaction but the reasons are wrong.

Can you imagine that? A recognition shock stumbles over system and details
the confusion of waking up by the smashed frame.
Long walks beneath enamel moons. A scrabbling at the interior.
The edgy constancy of nerves and wet stares,
I can see it from the root to the stem. My vision is terrible.
Could you wake for anything more? You know where it all comes from.
You? I could have seen the memory coming.
Magic words never make any sense. Infinitudes alive to the dead hours.
Tortures in their proper places. Speech.

It happens, when it opens the drawer of your clean and nameless voice.
What you imagine is fringed in dentistry and nailed to music
and splattered into the social. Me too. Or then teeth in my fist.

Everyone (you) spoke the language just as good. Can you imagine that?

## *The Origins of Love and Hate*

Cross-grained dark
falls to a lost gasp

high-stepping irony floods
from television screens

particles of being invaded
regroup in a soft aura

against the light of years
choked by perennial systems.

Open another window, and another
as yet such brilliant flower-heads ghost

in misted focus played
out on the boards

all the faces turn to each & laugh
huskily in the playbacks

witness to the artless cranesbill
of mellow self-deception

and sleeping half-life,
exposure too good for me

though what the barren hillsides
were for otherwise I can't imagine.

## *Late Capital*

Not much light
left nostalgia
instead of hair
both sides of the cloud
multiple lost
end collapsed
run round and round
in furry darkness
buttered up for
special treatment
oil in the ear
in a compact
a freewheeling approach
he said, he said it
in a voice like wet fur

## *Irreducible Blue*

Still day extends the line
and cajoles the bows in harmony
across the bone, across the street
a sign of life stopped the bike
or am I only romanticising
a simple journey to an end
suddenly in view and never out of it
now and in the singing night
and the singing dawn
your tiring grace so present
these terrible times
to have an attack of heart
and jump down from the blazing roof
all rescued from the frantic calm
of not writing by Surprise and Inspiration
as I may be sworn
I'll do it, whatever it is,
because of you. This isn't it
yet it is what I have tried
to make of it, again
and again, typing against the bone
chorus sweetly deaf in life
as the leaves return
they bide their time at night
in a fire of worry before the early milkman
calls across the street
with reassurance for the guttering
flame of verse that seeks
a way to ease and hand you into it.

## *Speaking of Life*

Frail dust in the bloodflow
not answering the door behind my eyes

some fracas stifles a cry at every corner
plaster images crumble and vanish

I wanted to shake off your presence
and I got lost on the way here

I thought someone was following me
but it was all there was to me when I arrived

to deface the picture of a man
without taking his feet off the ground

## *Prattle*

Close darkness warms
my skin towards the thought
of you that keeps
flowing as my heart
keeps going as bodies
seem to I can lie
to myself to sleep

## *You Never Said*

Don't say the light's going
shadows growing as the wind gets up
and owls at the gate

Don't say the dead hours are out again
beating at the shutters
like a heart with serious doubts

Don't say anything that sounds like a word
breaking over the track under winter branches
beside a deaf person with milky eyes

Don't say what's up
wasting night after night
monitoring the death of sunlight

Don't say too much about the past
things you loved bleeding all round the house
moments when years suddenly freeze.

## *Time How Short*

*There is a Moment in each Day that Satan cannot find,*
*Nor can his Watch Fiends find it: but the Industrious find*
*This Moment & it multiply, & when it once is found*
*It renovates every Moment of the Day if rightly placed.*
— William Blake

### I. RED PRIEST

As in cotton frocks and bicycles
barley trembles in the moody, wonderful air

What we walk in not a photograph
clenched in other desperate hands
slowly the air thickens

Rain not anywhere still
in this passionate suspense

## II. INTERFERENCE

Listen, what I don't say
or could deny the words mean
lines of scruple or waste
the merest roof
to hear winds
burning river of ignorance
reluctant to mean
to the crime of sound
or mind to reach reason
then swept out of the frame
heels flaming on the stones
of the site of this
this poor rendering
to say the least

## III. MATTER AND MEMORY

Cloudy morning slides across today's indecision
everything's on my side except my veil
of nerves my vanity and speaking clock
encased in earlier images and untrue versions

I speak you wait something indecipherable
slowly changing masses shade into grey
softened by yellowish suggestions of budding leaves,
bring out a momentary shadow on the slates

coldly erased; bitter weeping within sight
down corridors of unabandoned nature;
violets are mine, nature is blue, roses are like
a red, red pool

Likeness is not like a landscape, a
tract of fertility or menace laid
over brows of hulls in wide brown clarity
and shadow: the moment repeats and repeats.

## IV. APROPOS

A sundial in dawn mist
defining the virtues
what is a garden?

Shadows thought
a beech tree
nostalgic common sense

Spinning dreams in
later backdrop
the legislative wheel

These images are
thrown up in silhouette
on wild eyes

All this sadness
has orbital courses
not by way of despair

I must need
tremor of language
this isn't opaque

Anything musical
a minimum
eager for an absolute

In the split second
no more material
continues to unfold

I embrace you
this isn't opaque
it's autumn.

II

Rain blows against the glass
there is an absent figure
in this composition

Leaves and water represent
slammed doors, hisses of breath
drenched in social relations

Rapid and insistent jabs of thought
like pigeons' necks on the platform
I would like the time please

Then the great relief of motion
with a purple-brown sweep of michaelmas daisies
in an abrupt light

Don't take your eyes off me
burning like the Alexandra Palace
on a horizon

Unproductive solitude
can be figured as rapid white paint marks
as flat as a wooden surface

You know this as it is spoken
it reveals a true moralism
I fall in with it straight away

Sleep or no sleep
the bristled skyline is stained
with hope to see my pilot face to face

How come primroses are out
beneath heavy branches of sloes
like a transparency of history?

## VI. TIME HOW SHORT

Voices like mosquitoes slant
past glasses
towards a dormer window
the fading pink light
claiming loudly it was the best
I could possibly have
so ist das Jahres Ende
I suppose similar people
drinking in a more consciously Scottish attitude
otherwise glazed in national inertia
shut up in a little room like this
all those years and the syringa or the buddleia
out of sight round the corner
occasionally a painted lady at the glass
or a peacock like a spirit returning to earth
or rather leaving it
as figures leave the shops to pattern wet streets
speaking for all of them in autumn
as time consumes itself in our society
and we consume its exile in our hearts

## VII. FAR AND AWAY

The fault mine
in lifted air caught in midday
impermeable behind the eye
like a page missing
to enforce a lie

or a man writing letters for work
banging against the door
against cold within a thing to hold
and hold, as pretty as gold
just lying about every day

thorns and wire make a last ditch pretty
cast shadows on nodules of flint

jaded light approaches cancellation
the desire of the mouth for the scar

## VIII. NO RESOLUTION

Hold fast to
fast as
the changing sky

my square of window
changes shape
as if my eyes could fly

living on the edge of
hearing from you
under the same crowds

gentlest democracy
how hard you are
like a simple truth dismissed

## *The Night The*

bark abandoned on the night air
a distant recension by small creatures in a ditch
and an owl's crisp echo by the library

*

some
people are sleeping
mouths fused by indifference
and blank tickets to symbolic realms

*

mendacity?

*

stocks rise,
shuttered primroses
by the ground
ignore the commander-in-chief

*

some things never sleep
it's the TV counterpart
you hear too much about
in other terms

*

dead stone writers speak to ears of corn
and cloudbanks over Suffolk
and all that necessary oil
in the air

*

before first light
leaden with cultural determinism
breaks as self-defence
on a million radios,
morally refuelled wakefulness
takes many forms
and we are all possessed.

# *Postcards to Spain 1986*

1. A NOTE ON AIR AND MOTIVES

As unexplained, for the most part,
mere melody revolves in loops
of class and cloud: yet persons sing in pain

and wonder at their lives out loud.
This was the basis of so much, motive
even, and absorbed a great deal of attention

against which, for example, there was the swelling
sound of the Thaelmann Brigade singing
as they marched. It cheered some people up.

Listen, don't worry, even about rust
and bills; it's a sharp possibility
that anything human may change

and the edge of song may be a razor
or a hedge of song erasing
unwanted lines of music from ordinary vistas.

## 2. CODA

That was a brigade of men.
There were no women in it
in that version of a war
as often happened.
However, women are not the meat in a vegetarian diet.

## 3. POINT BLANK FUTURE

The same day the wall cracked as if it was a sign of life
the same day was a voice in the air, falling quietly
the same day was a petition obscuring its intention
the same day I opened a tin and it was full of tiny marching children
the same day you spoke for hours I think
the same day hung over us all in cloud like blankets
the same day the meaning of marble escaped us
the same day was a voice in the dark
the same day I discovered necessity they killed Lorca
the same day is never unspoken unless by imaginary beings
the same day they were all *voluntarios de la vida*
the same day I went I came back
the same day abandoned by olive-green water
the same day shook with anger every time I passed it
the same day was a sudden tremor in the dry ground
the same day is a ghost of itself that you just catch a glimpse of
the same day is actually the fabric of society
the same day gazes out of your eyes as gazes out of mine
the same day we look up and see arching or should that be searching?
the same day we may not want to be in this
the same day is the song that never rose from a million throats
the same day is not final, not the last word
the same day rang all day like a telephone
the same day won't call you, dear proletariat
the same day was the voice of an unwritten stone

## 4. WISH YOU WERE HERE

Imagine a band of fire to play
grey-blue clouds across an early death
in streets where any number of hearts waltz
in careless love, loving the emerging leaf
and smoking visions, the atmosphere
of May
            and wouldn't leave it
for the tingling blade of a word or two
from you. Who would? As the venomous jets
that bind our ears
and the radioactive wind that softly sweeps
to a statement blind to the depths of balding sorrow
cement the justified moment
like revolving futures in a matte shot
from an open door.

Take it again from here: my life rioted
at the light of dawn in my pocket, at the phrase,
at the overtime chorus of the fertile land
as it stops for the shout of Spain
whatever that was
on a train in the night
as it holds the wheel from inside
rny spinning mouth, my Huesca, my Molesworth,
my companions, my bases in the altered light
of the world's outpouring!

Oh corn and guest and bell and summer field
if you should tum up again
feel free to stand by the vanished English line
till an operator gives you the international exchange
and you get through and hear the dazed clicks
of an integrated system on a life-support machine.

## *Postcard to Italy*

At times the land's edge whitens into tidal debris
lolling under the early light
as relenting curves of sleep suck at the pebbles

and shards of warbling dream are suddenly revealed
fading into sand in case the rational grasp
turns over too heavily into a coloured injury

such as memory could be made out to be until the full light
screens the olive trees inland by the moment
and cars drive fast down all the curvy roads

establishing daytime tracks beside the longing grasses,
the reading knowledge of a language.
I think here, I am not making music like the faithful cuckoo

among the alien streets lit by yesterday's trading figures
ne l'ora che comincia i tristi lai
la rondinella presso a la mattina...

The shadow that I was asleep shortens into the day
I hope to have: absence hanging like the amber warmth
of a sun across my path to provide a note of laconic solvency

as I shave. The thought of your face fills the glass
at once like heat echoing on a red hillside
to dance over the silvering like a deceptive vision

or erase a wind solo rising like smoke to disperse
night before I want it to, water in the basin clouding
as the day will here, later, as the air thickens in token.

## *A Reading*

Silvered glass. Approach a person. Hover in thought.
Flick at the catch, stammer in German,
about the burning sky and its helmsman
in dead shadow.

            It was a flame between each finger
in every heart that heard her words,
a memory of the structure of the 'as'.

The further glass stands unframed still
against the columns, the image unopened,
being little more than it ever was, but there
to care about the desperate calm
and virtual person lying in the light.

## *L'Histoire*

Flames cloy the traverse
work appeals for
means by
a silence
inside each egg of day
would venture out
with a shawl
from beside the self
towering against a prison
like an azure poison
pinned across the right
by the right of way

It was one voice
they spoke with
don't tell me
they were poor
they danced
& used to tiptoe
by the prison
when the moon was red
like a fated harvest
curling in the air.

## *Small Changes*

As fades the tractor homeward
and folded day tilts
to a vacant field and beams
from the image of a house

So colour returns to a small
refugee moon
and a musical evening begins
downing a quick one

Before the glass reveals
a remodelled nose, and from the mouth
if a voice then a voice
of exacter pitch

On such tethered scale
the music burns up
in a classic image
of third-world melancholia

What the eye can't see
in a fanciful sieve
of starry empathy
won't do no good my dear

Unflapped pastoral maybe
let slip or caught
by a bow incomplete then
under the arc of charity.

## *Guinea on China*

Don't let spaces, budding lines
drop cracked on to the red margin.
The isle of plenty is a communal dream
but not if, don't forget, the cost is
not too much soft leather

In the bar, salty saucers, how dated
zinc would be! Take a computer, bad head,
in low gears after the missile trailer
winking red. Go home and go to bed.
The last wore out the question
beneath the misty moon.

Don't turn your back on animal faces
I took him to mean. There's no sense
in the original green folder. I love you
as webs drift and whitewash. Reform.
I never heard so much lost breath.

## *High Time*

Light breaks window
cats shiver
road works wink
in a steady consensus
hurting like a necklace
set press to wear it
and pass into the opera
radiant gabble
saying nothing personal
at breakfast
the course of true love
a first course in not dying
or going mad
in the shops
so bipolar activity leads to
a short and happy clasp
such as we can feel
at the back of the neck
to transcribe this shining information
as it comes
in spite of the clear tide
years peak out
the ruffled sand flattens
and a misty line
of rust unseals a touch
of friendly eye-contact
and keeps going
like a voice on the line
I want to hear occasionally
to be hit in the brain
as the day comes back

we all do, we need this
text of memory
renewed by radiant states
flagged and reflagged in new growth
from low on the imperial stem
for all the shadowy exercises
in the nocturnal mirror
of another power we watch
newspaper pasted
over our eyes.

## *The First Intervention*

Last light floats past the black trees.
Another dollar. A great bill and a force
for change. It definitely falls to one another

to read Russian, to say nothing of this
kindly moment or that. Surfacing between my teeth
it felt like a language, a bitter phone

you love to use in slow motion curtain,
that voice reconstituted in blue on blue
as our capital sells its skin for time out of mind

and sustains us on the edge of talk, grey
absent or annulled, to the core
streaming out loud across the entire space.

# *When It Seemed That All Was Lost*

Some sleeping head reclining in a different spirit
dreams in amber and glass against all time to come
eyes closed to the kind flux of light and likeness.

The light cuts hard buildings around us, shadow
conniving with sweet rhythms and hot food to shape
ideologies, snapped and dotted into every heart.

So the dearest future creatures beneath the sun set down and loved
with a purpose
to outrun any fingered lapels on a light-weight suit
imagined the scene and ran it, hiding behind newspapers in a small
café.

Where a new journey was a defined shadow on the driest martini,
like the light of tyranny sharply bleeding off earlier contemplation
poured back so the mask keeps its humane appearance.

What we would buy is gone deep within us like a hanging thought
and projected like an old dove on to our silly retinas
in a fashionable curtain print to keep the world at bay

While pudgy fingers deal in sleep futures on a grand scale
and the time is destitute because it lacks the web of names it is,
and how it is concealed and revealed and trafficking those coins.

The sleeping body turns at this point, muttering words
from the communards, advertising financial services buttered up for
the taking
and sleeps on in darkness, for the world like a quietened bestowal.

# *Solo*

Basal options are deleted by the things
he done and how they could never augment
kindly note and burn the novel, like indoor fireworks
extruding weightless narrative as it goes up
in smoke. The rest is doing us good on the cards
so they introduce a policy review for clustered
antipathy and idleness promising crisp vision
tomorrow. But it's not a matter of luck
they've screened such humdrum cries out at the terminal
to reduce shock at the new South East, it's
dead behavioural, ministers lying there in white
parole. Hearing voices is getting commonplace.
The shot tower was one refuge from reaching hands
though the smell was no way smart, not with the sun
up there all day. Solo wants help. Pages and pages
of typescript under grey ash, can you hold
or call again thrice on the social fund.
At times argot shows through brittle speechifying
to release a little comfort for the papers, attacks the heart
casually and tosses it into ragged robin. Then
the spectacle continues an attractive prospect
and at the same time avoids payment.
The delegation walked right through a strip search
like they had bags on their heads,
on soft leather, pink hands clutch the option
to develop as a matter of crafty units
chained to the day, like lunch. A researcher did the writing
and it dissolved all memory, till the white bodies
lay at the subway entrance, or rocked on their stumps,
completely bandaged in the quiet light. Canvas
stories hang and defy vision in a virtual flick

of his head on the button as if it was ever so. Solo refuses sleep
and spreads over the land on automatic drill,
a virtual factor chalking on the odd wall of death.

# *Wherever a Head*

Wherever a head appears through flesh in a glassy extrusion of fond
ignorance svelte with immaculate novelty and covered against weeping,
to find something crackly at the fingers' end would be a polity
in miniature, some hyperbolic but dark-suited absence stepping down
from an official car and its sheeny populist vision.

On the other head be it, the official crown of weeds and old mortar
running down to the nape where the dream convulses in lung disease
sucking the pebbles back in the throat as the dated tidal
lyric stemmed by sun voting predictions takes its place in every
bedside anthology of lost or executed souls.

This eye bedizened with puzzling, what can you expect? Such random
stock hammered deep into the lease creates a loud humming across
pretty plastic tables, such perfect teeth scavenging the burger
for hot pickle traces, when they do lie too much for tears
glistening on poppy and meadowsweet stalks the headlines say.

For what they say is equally the case and thus flares up
from day to day. Habit. Imagine there are four movements in all
and practise them in several languages. What would there be to love
most? Heavens above, I don't need to tell you how to long
for absent social beauty. He was a lovely entertaining speaker.

Deep end days and nights have their stars and blotto vagaries
from one word to the next she says holding well on a wet surface
but might as well have trusted to luck. No time was so oiled
or palm lines so believed or so run by martial options.
They cut the price, you see, and just loved the issue.

Returning to black and white a screen flickers over the sea
and we listen to a story that there is neither we nor I in
so the sentences are ploughed back leaving arms under the sodden
soil belt. Slender chance called upon steps lightly under the rain
and the most pitiful stumps beckon and sprawl perversely.

Fear might abate the volume of attentive imagery in a flurry of paste
on the tongue. All I could hear was some state of being
but it's good to have ears at all. The air is full of water.
Grooves and cavities inspire language from street to street
as they always did, body and paper, as light goes on and off.

# *The Name of Day*

You pay to go in, you act
on information
and to break the ice you die
a hero. Block the door
if you are so anxious
as an attic charm
from the dead
and unscripted returns
through all eternity
in an eyebrow.

Teeth flush to china
bats cavort and rise again
& fade on wings of thought
because of the mirror.
It fails the sense, becomes
inert and brushed as light on a pebble
wet by sea or rain.

No state to be in
like blue lines
on the willow scar by the pipes
coming together in a shelly wetland
courtly song and dance.
We don't amount to nothing
like the movies' sacred finery,
the blinder blindness of a phrase
about a day in my pleasant land
specked with fragments
of strategy in a ditch.

There's more to fear where this comes from.

## *Say Nothing*

Envied light
glittery leaf
flattens out
disordered hope

nettle words
on all my skin
black water
can't quite hear

a virtual grid
frames each gust
billows inward
in sudden grey

take out the bone
to play down
fallen webs
local acts of

arranged trees
in binding twain
by clock time
set fast

no rash acts
as symptom
simply nothing bears
renewal up

we are in line
to shadow falls
of will, we owe
more than it says

# TENSE FODDER

*Equipage*, 1993

*Nous n'avons pas une voix seulement pour parler, mais aussi pour faire silence.*
— Jean-Louis Chrétien

# *A Bit Apart*

Vanity and clumsiness will not be lvric
fodder as they inhere or blaze forth

just qualities in the mutagenic pall
breathed in by mothers with shut windows

and long strokes of grey bestowing politics
like a management buy-out of the Habsburgs

the grey veers into push-button metaphor
an effective strategy review for the eastern outlook

(in Chancellor Kohl's punitive liberation
Arbeitslosigkeit macht frei)

modelling provides a new point of view for the imaginary
a harlequinade of futures in black and white

it disintegrates before our eves
described as a glaring example of the gulf between

hope and hold. always selling one against it
or making representations (if I thought

how could a mountain be secret? if space shrinks
so much won't the words conspire?)

but looking across the chemical works from this sealed window
at the lank birds dropping like dandruff

I think they are representing loss of speech.

## *Look Back*

I low poplars froze crisply
against the light. Orange.

Observers don't lift fingers.
To lips. A sticky idealism

over a vista of nice times.
Watch as you curl up inside

with a story made to a formula
of natural matters.

Only on completion of the news
from tiptoe to freedom as more news

in fact as the truth came
though shot at willingly.

Now that it's warmer you can take
a jersey off without lucky prices

on the books that look so new
and yet without which it is not sustained .

When I move my eyes
the upheaval is apparent

these are my several fields
the path lies under them, intense

and hazy under frost or columbine.
History never abandons itself.

## *Lino Cut*

So many mothers haul the fat engine of day
up the s haft and cook the awful flesh

letting go some corporate intuition of our history
sits ill on a flawed window sill

and still a stubble-faced memory burns
spades and suddenly attacks the newspaper

stokes the columns for a war
and brings the geraniums in for movement

a thinking red. Go or go. Did you find
acid pain on what page? Each leaf curls as I think

so I don't feel no pain in the dark
but I don't breathe symbols anyone can hope

to nearly cluster over the usual London spot
in a box. how can you be so kind?

I try to read another person's words
wood lip round time chamfered for safety

only pines bound to a short life among courted
sentences from San Diego to anywhere else you like

tell their own story and won't be some purge
in material death, no more quick dance

to tell you the shift in space is all
there is if you want us to continue the search.

## *The Garden Party*

Committed to daylight did this to me
used it to poison air water and the soil

no heroism or bomb-throwing
just objects recurring in modified modes

green as any known idle reverie
questions are recorked for tomorrow's sacrifice

original skin hums as if to extend
me against a different background

writing in the border with an inky pen
no scent of marjoram, no arbiter of time

these shadowy English beds exploit hope
to preserve value and misery and no alternative

is silent in the will of shade where fathers
hammer vocabulary to induce dreams of purpose

going for broke in some ludicrous home
putting a distant hand in the transparent air.

Hide the tree, conceal personal distress
wear and take off clothes in a blind bracket

and vanish as I speak. I can't understand strangers
but they're the somatic death I'm travelling into

After I've gone don't fizzle out drinking bottles
in the shower that falls from the unbreathed sky

write or cut shades of my name in the bark
and ring retraction with a hard colloid edge.

## *Sleep*

Looking for it. What I absorb from a bank
is meaning something I don't want to like
and need to love outside the borrowed life
to be worked off and forgive and forget.

If I knew what the absence was it would be
orange against the grass in the rain. Yes
and too heavy to lift, reserved for us,
a vision passed on, a sum to expect.

Not there. No story. Ingesting something
eight years old during the night
looking for some doorway into the dark
my balance has o'erstepped my will

and nettles catch my skin instead of
fair outlook switchback nausea
projects the outside of buildings
in the same recursive pattern over development plans

longer and longer shadows search abroad
for what I love I forget to light,
what being proper stories hates to be
will not be refunded.

The cubists painted other fronts too
leaving the bill as nature, looking sweet
inside a monument to eating in public
and arrested investigators of fraud

for fraud in the story still looking for
something good in the story of the resistance
of glass to stone as the outer ripple
eats the rest like a photocopier.

## *This and That*

From that time onwards I believed
a small painting of a subject
flung back what the silence wished
and did not obtain

For years I lived in common with it
and spines on shelves
welling up like a kind of milk
which it does not matter

In terms of interchange I was
a few steps down the street and back
in a denim jacket for my given body
a hard and fast label is the thing

Which of course the phone confirms
and shrouds me over and poisons
life all night in case of technology
all right rhetoric

Dreaming full of live weight
of conviction that instates the realm
looked out through glass at the
full moan of the singing air

Unwise to walk by
or gloss the muddiness of words
once in existence
shifting by dint of surprise

I'd come and go at any price
but I'm beyond it:
then it rains then stops and
then the blackbirds again.

What will warn us of our disposal?
certainly not prose or bits of paper
photocopies piled up and stapled
and doubtless more arduous etc.

Who writes something new
that sets no limits
to dwelling or dawning
or telling or mourning

Painfully sewn in complete
silence made visible
by small holes in the folds
between this and what it says.

## *No Contact*

Think of the dark falling too much and be angry, some reflex
incentive and they sit back and do nothing in a lather

killing a few for the cameras but the red sand and the rocks
fade as the air heats up and slithers out of the shade.

Bare voices. Not even mine
probably off the radio talking about the economy

ringing in the new light grey layers of ash
and future shape of blarneying puppetry

I can hardly call it waste or political aesthetic
or shopping around like blood in vacancy

armed with psychotic birds gaping
and gasping for derivation, it's gone

here and now and forever. No cut, no finish
recursive ink narrating a single case, a recent case.

What did he do? I'll tell you what he did
or hindered even a few flowers and their sweetness and troubles.

How some casual reach bludgeoned the mouth
for want of an intenser care

and the dazed function of colour
just bled off into unrectified threads

blown about by the breath of a few words.

A want of all the virtues had remained intact
as the airport or the market

sniping at fish and coffee in their safe little
corridors of grief and promising days of late spring

attended by a vast audience, all unmoved. I thought
something else once in a European country, watching the almond tree.

Some fathers, some mothers, given up in a circle
for a kinder pain, hate these keen objects

and their lazier dreams of substitution
in case of pulling the strings alike

and even cry generously for another aptitude to a name
but what can they buy for a betrayed ornament?

Punish a few, kill a few and wade back out of the shallows
cradling a fish. Is that so cruel?

You could call it the national question after all
and beg it to stop. You could call it her wish for a child.

A slow drip or a ripple of severity
striating naked backs in the treasury

smothered each smile in blindness,
figured the stupid, and I didn't notice.

Walking in the streets openly
I have no-one to blame but myself

and still fail to vanish. What you call
an ignoble world is an open question.

The planes fly low over the present trappings
and fade loudly away. No contact.

Another concealed entity of restless embargo
has disinfected a far landscape

if we can decipher the dots properly.
This effigy is speaking again

and signs of resistance leak into the air.
There is an exceptional glow fuelling it.

## *These Days*

Flat out on a council argument
lost as a pencil, guarded as a résumé

it's true it was nothing deep
just a person in trousers

moments of a life swoop
even eat out of her hand

crumbs of mental storm
played twice in the same key

looking for the checkout
to classify some trace of being

more than being and less than anything
in green and blue ordinary life

swelling up and splitting for history
into a pair of opposites

my girlish heart rearranges
the long and the short

to prospect for all the lost boys
lugged through the meal

resources of entropy call my
bluff mannerisms to renounce

slow motion advertising conduits
of carnage by plastered lack

and then come back and fall to the ground
at the frontiers the glass

areas of time full of implicit
regret for designated readings

and still hoping for a moment
of street light to shape

odd words into sentences suspended
until written down the side

of stung and planted ground
from the homeless feet up

to the vast mouth it crams
with nobody's utopian shadows

obviously needing credit
from time to time.

## *The Wire*

Crueller ones all hearts enchaining
sit under a tree in the afternoon

wondering what to obey. Internally
they are us in the currents

that sweep us into the idea
of years of paid labour

slipping into pockets
in regard to sex for example

photographing streets
in unconscious investigations of painting

all surfaces sheened by the rain
on a winter evening

bumping against light skies
wanting the impossible illness

this idiot revenge strokes
my face and wipes away my hope

a fine collusion sets store by
any rate it can get

divided by and thus creates
a world of awkward mental life

pending imagined faults
against some indifference

beneath revolving painted air
my little brother, my son,

my unattained and certain boundaries
emitted as quasi-military release

from torn or flashing want
to be at hand as bright as an adept gaze

at local deaths blinkered
by dancing fires

mythic amplitude trapped in a wire
certainty of tumbling dusk

as if my life depended on it.

## *Less and Less*

What you haven't got I imagine
hollowed out like in a fever

in mist over ploughed fields
we saw something on the bench bound up

making it a figure with notes
suggestive of committal

circles behind the coarse effect
making a noise like speech

a gestalt image deflects the camera
arrangement from the normal window

such a surprise the last object
promptly brought a reminder

for poorer states and regions
where the mother's life was rejected

only to be expressed as a joke
along the railway line

colour was cut from magazines
with a residuum of death

their value may increase in Africa
but to have a heart

I have to be in pain or separation
distance varying in length

from different linguistic des ire
and spilled coffee

half a life continuing the social poetry
she called them tributes

to the rhythmic shadows of
the very act of this world

and I call it a game with sticks
by grasping it and any system

to make sense without end
a possible world war

like some sort of bank
for intersubjective transactions

I'm certain it was a field
with tinned food and stunted trees

everyone knows what to do
when they go crazy

they write a long digressive poem
on the balcony and wait for trains

hurtling through loss of interest
to quote at some length from local usage

resting by the fiercest negatives
to help cope with the same time

in the midst of thick columns of smoke
and leaving matters at that.

## *Facing Page*

Vision unrolls vertically
based on a sphere pressed flat at meeting

looking ahead to a time
to offer dispersed meanings

well coded construction rates
a strange list of comfort

visible in country of origin
as local expenditure buds

cutting loot from right to left
long past nightfall

masks in the stash
in body order face oblivion

with his mother tongue
his most fluent encounter with money

a literal beginning in the eyes
of bright green cultural property

so little or no vestige
cut to an honorary degree

to the dealer behind the writer
be sure of a concealed hand

wash out your ears if you want
to set foot in the same door

your skin a hostage to bits of dust
from life still to come

healing slowly away
met off a stopping train after Royston

everything can end in songs
filling mouths with torn work

shed as piecemeal calm by terms
you dare not touch in the morning

or observe the slight figures
driven into a corner by blood and language

open to visitors *au plan juridique*
clustered gaze on the hoardings

still no sign of resistance to
the taste of food destroying its name

you can get it in tiny orange threads
called linkage. Why not be day-neutral?

No need for a spoke in the right
moment called the end

if I can so express it
called a cover version of fission

a floating glass threshold
leaves the enclave without sleep

anyone who cares to take a white powder
can write the first two acts

or a tender scene with a bit of time
slipping into a crude mark appraisal

the shadow of the press text
obscures the title

tense before and after death
in the eventual play of hungry roots

sell starry gaps between illusions
of a service economy and backwash

refuse to stick with plausible sedatives
so the dog only confirms the limit

the loss is absolute from several habitats
not just in the sky

an illegible privacy set up all over Europe
in a fine type of public disgust

believing in objects
is deranged

turn to page seven
for the photo of another face.

## *Drying Out*

More about spoke down nothing but
nice in dust and despatches

my homily moments on the wheel
fined each of them twenty pounds

on the spot. These daft sequels
sang bravely, heaved over the wall

round the spine, badly afraid of
dying out of all proportion to the light

forms of reversal into sponge. What the day
brings forth as image of the past homage

fades at once, threshold of general satisfaction
in the plan of the central station

call it what you will, pronounced
shudder. Petit-bourgeois red meat fanciers

with their ways of life adored the
scattered flakes of cloud cover

miners and all who set out the same camp
come down to a breath of orange

without title, sex or character
revised since above, free as the rabbits

of the garrigue underfoot, storms
abridged attempting to be substantial

zero I for another glass please
but read hopscotch in the works of time

that final window an emblem on the pavement
is brought home to any imaginary weapon

legal web for certain powers of real food
split open and vomiting fine dust

over the table. Moscow print washes out
as if accidentally faced in order

the relief drum a dedicated thing to die of
any time you see it. Now you don't.

# MUCH MORE PRONOUNCED

*Equipage*, 1999

---

*The enigma [of depth] consists in the fact that I see things, each one in its place, precisely because they eclipse one another, and that they are rivals before my sight because each one is in its own place.*

*— M. Merleau-Ponty*

*It is, after all, our very uncertainty about their seriousness that makes it possible for ghosts to continue to affect us.*

*— Jonathan Elmer*

## *Some Title*

Basic flame stands in yellow fog as copse
or corpse logging functions in the distance
of the general earth, a charred mill stands
out of narrow time roundly offered over
dim followers at war with the faces often
recognised. Stake ripped in the heart of
us, from elders on, or a blind or a lamp dew
on grass flickering to dying out can only re-
cord what it won't forget until after a sleep.

Come over all the bridge nightingales, go
for the acorn hue, jeopardise thrill to a dull
ochre. Drop infancy holdings from another
long night of vertiginous collapse, give her
a renewed taste for life and tidy up and cook
it. Clean the primal stove, looking up. Opt
for thinking under grids and over tasty this
and that function as if, say, a stone to be pro-
nounced or put in the way of how it turns out.

In another naughty hit a couched delphic feeling
does not transform any animal in a letter
to thy hart. The jug, the bowl, the impasto
is my retyred minde, you find it out at a long
laugh scorning all the cares of famine, fabric
choice driven from skies and hedges into normal
bin end searches for even a lark. Say what you
hear, the light has gone and detach and expel
take their place as überwords conjoined to us.

Let me put this out. Though roses flag and dip
in dark memory, stress disrupts their prosody
from one to the other and ever back again in
September, where dash is tied down to handle
with care, or if you wish and drop suddenly
out of sight, death. Set this to come and go and
swallow it down until it clips a lie like a peppery
olive rises in a mother clasp, all grist and iris
dresses. If it's old enough I'll pay to have it, truly.

I'll pray to have it, to make it clear within, and
contained with a mind to match. At the start of
this clue what but pain? Kingfishers for mental
concept of growth as opposed to even moral
sex in a chair, as he would say, how sad after the
reading yet another transformation of the part.
Pinch is destroyed, warm feelings, colour gummed
up and over views of treacly Sunday dissent. Go
down and see, answer the door, step after step.

Drawn by the very worst for what? Wear? Huddle
of erosion may help as if listening also describes
a frame of open doors and windows, if there is a
sense of movement perhaps even found to matter.
Kelp bed and west wind, cries of a pen in various
ways of treating me just kind of melt the flora of
exile. Play is implored by the bank whereon the time
expires in Latin letters, the break comes naturally
if the ringing is exact enough to grow on the shore.

# *Much More Pronounced*

Don't we really want
the cranks of nine
black cap of piquant set
in little ivory sombrero
at my wit's end?

Here we have radiant doll
in an old bag of ready catch
mellow bead wrist to pull
with wired devotion
as her screen image

I didn't like to look
out of it, slogan treated as
it is wonderful to hear
all tricked up and vapid
and acclaimed our censors said

Or didn't we? Slice trivial
squeaks of nations, reel times
buzz off arid and plain
holding a weapon in each
other art and rock with mirth

Really bottled England of twin
prophets by some ironic past
served a slim ordeal
as a sort of temple so I say
yes to her rag arms of refuge

A moth and t he knife boy
want stone about to step
forward for many of us
earlier the being masks
father wakes the point of it

To be ripped off with compliments
for the soul and made the outer
sound whistles and gasps
comprehend the crowds that look
over an art occupation

Like the task whose task is
all the other dead once more
augurs of this change will speak
the stones and our conceptions, yes
as a lip to scrap our witty person

A double fatal ground
owns life in other words
an exaltation we call love
for the person bearing it stumbling
about a panic pot label

His or mine? In the name
of the mistake
a question arises
alive in a split power hand
wrapped about that decadent thought

The best we can be under the sky
new data for a long negation
made from bad shape
natter on song and larval address
so get it down on real paper

What is to be dead? You get back
all residence on earth
and row me over a charmed life
you want to go somewhere
crowd to the front of the stage

Little red rooster refuse to plague
relics in a ruin of glass
hardly a definite proposal
fresh wind blowing fond of the state
and a little wine dry as a bone

The lake is wonderfully sad and quiet
black water as still as death
I have your kind note
there is nothing for it
as much as I like to hear

The catch is the voice run
on hypnotic images or
dolls on a plane if the ticket
to inner vision in a suave
nut-shell seemed wanting

A wish to indicate we can
bleach abstract thought to a dot
may invent details (he is
depressed, I was afraid of this) both
in an imperfect replica

Competing species of plant life
revamp urban fire drill
get more than they pay for
unease pressure from below
and fly in the face of art

Only the French and Chinese
cure in the brine waves
the obstacles being removed
in a golden fashion
and held in this light bowl

Having to be distant
he began a more complete account
for dust, damp, soot, mice and worms
when it was packed away
to do this till he was dead

Survivors of a family
if they mastered the emptiness
during the filming of this chance
yes I do understand your
untold stories that lie behind it

Cellophane heart I'm talking to
you and poetry after making your order
you won't hear from us
the best ways to use each one
come to those who wait

Hanging over our heads
a withering flash due to
regret cannot be renewed
blind as a battered case
of ever their mother had thought

Another shell cracks in helpful
pain drizzled with oil
and smeared with saline
solutions not to be had except
by the present itself

Unspeakable fair this silence
haunts me thus with feare
so I'm writing to tell you
miles before it's gone
in exchange for a living wager

A slightly open black gate
objectively new and yellow
a topaz mist going up like a shutter
to disclose too much acidity
coming now to hang on

To be rescued alone to advertise
writing to drive and drive
and end up with a life of bewildered
autobiography in muffled fabric
O baby what allure to a changing face!

I should ascribe the boundaries
of this country to awe
and eye to steeple
at a point where its sudden balm
slips off and is visibly enacted

Isn't it time that we were familiar with
the ultimate purpose of humanity?
Flowers, sea-shells, answers and chains,
artfully carved birds on the branches of trees,
what do poets praise more highly?

Nothing stops awash with blood
real fast as an egg. Post me it
to be what there is in the process
of it flavoured by trains
and their evocative night calls

Nothing but time to any of these
cold stars properties as questions
know that I'll want patents of
how life ought to be lived at night
thrown away like a country gesture

Shocks as fatal as toasting soap
a man poured and set over
windy ramparts thou art blind
as sheep at last your nape
in the clouds ajam with scudding

Fishing in sleep furniture
torrents of outer rafters
buy me lines mate and foam
boogy-woogy abstracts
in order to order this

A passage lamp somewhere else
faithful to that epoch
the journal jerks the strings of
scarf or socks or rags of time
to repair the grammar of music

So drive on past daffodils
made in the open mouth
in ink for the future
leaving it to the mercy of
my own fate my hand

Writing to remain alive as
something emptied into time
the balcony was something else
dyed in the wool of an awkward self
like a blue stain on stucco reason

Such white tunes burn
like nobody's business only
brackets hold us up here
and European languages spill out
of every literal appearance

To see or lapse into a happier state
was the art of the circus
all lucky legs and camels
to bring you satisfaction
or your money back

The fathers could then be
recomposed diegetically to
form a cycle or shared meaning
compatible with a system of
discounting by arguing too much

Not being able to crumple
as a block when things get difficult
information requires amendment
I would be grateful if you could
let me know this as soon as possible

At night the joint fears minimum
tales of backstreet tariff ways
to request a value for money
or tiptoe like trees along
the canal miles from the market

By accident her arm grew
darker than the future was
because they had no choice with
great anxiety flavoured with salt
as a prime exchange paradigm

She thought the answers were slight
objects like lapis allergies shackled
to first return of a mother's terror
hiding her peak intonation as
functions that fate has dealt us all

Beginning at five not in fact Jewish
edges of the sea should invite distaste
at the printed words coalition
of clustered or prickly scraps of landscape
to loop evenly up covering the shells

So it was voice mainly as despatches
from the given waves of serotonin
in a continual buzz of self leakage
on to deterrent maxims waved about
flat-out remedies for denying anything

Gleaming above the porch the idea
of providing a floor battled the moths
in grim theory shadowed by Schutzbund
fantasies and weakened by two fungal
growths and a new corporate logo

If such a new dome of time
and transparent distance wraps
it all up with a compressed attachment
quickly take up a corn-flower
or hop to the darker shadow glitch

The eye and a pure delight in the
topics piece and slip forced from the sea
to be shot and stuffed for academic
frisson but on balance a fear of being
alone would say its images bluntly

Suppose her her head positive
but even more simple reader
the spectacle I might be too weak
not chic these dared to hope for
turns new moral access of heroic size

This forthright dream is style
at your feet in dayglo fronds and
speaks vivid walls confronting the
old traces to adorn the wolf
days unless you'd rather not

The white bear drifting across
the chain of her grandfather
like a winsome speedwell
might nominate the time of
aspen betrayal that we show

And cash it in without
hyperbole or incompletion
just at the edge of salt objects
under the tongue
sucking the Labour Party Manifesto

And so lash will to substance
at the bar impending some
diffusive wrack of silk
bother against massy clouds
and farewell strips of tissue

How can you talk like that?
phantom trio of early life
sleep in some coddled past
look back at the target fish
swept up in tragic kitchen practices

Listen to the rhythm of the
forming raid on the inartistic
cloths of grief: charred entities
laid neatly out, their lines
bundled into a noise of weeping

Feel little or nothing of the cause
my sole thought, watch the birdie
eat the lamb by the fell. By
the fallen understand
nothing but black and more black

Mother tongue plight in short
change is solid and durable
the dolly in the copper
a surprise to the memory
like a line of wet battery jars

Step up to my second question
in tangible words such as
what is the chance of
asking how you could say
something like that

A late afternoon myth
tangles in the entity's small flame
mouth open in sudden death
and fair lines. Used to
is a defective verb

Novel thought is too long
gone to be netted
I now realise and what resembles
analogy is layered in passing
time to its other domain

It's all anaphora now
threatening the system. Can't you
see it again and combine the terms
in a veranda with a view to
an outcome by autumnal beeches?

Pruning leaves traces that grow
semantically past first in a
version of democracy. A grid
underlies as what lies outside
growing up through it would if it could

Some secret agency passes for time
if the same applies to words
with only a slight thickening
in the black cap experienced
as a bitter maxim about standards

To collapse is not enough
to die from the same coin:
the same system to defeat itself
falls sharply as winter comes on
in an imaginary landscape

Piquant screen time on a light
breeze stay on the other hand
go out of this body
effracted into endless
bavardage instead of seeking

Which raises instruments of a
concrete whistle and does
eventually speak out
good visions in the air
so that this turns proverbial

Feet on the ground glass turn
and run for a hefted lark
as when to outstrip occult
funny business would turn heads
in true and in trim filade

Less than that time for
food cannot displease any man
burned up across the water
until all of animated nature
is as good a tactic as not at all

Across the plain a proleptic
cascade remains to be seen
under patches of reddening
light and carpathian distances
the wine is thin and confected

Spatial memory-traces of the
timing of tactile stimuli make
cortical maps that precipitate
more internal wilderness when
the whole array is moving

Why on earth is a serious
thing and the chalk-lines
closer rippled or ready to
come and hallucinate it
pronounced unspeakable

Maintained my grip like a leaf
out of time or perhaps
visionary for detail in our
matrix to complete the trope
say a rift in the irony map

Of course a cap on the cable
is not the same as culture when
we wrap a kind of puppeteer
bursting a history of this point
into that remarkable word amiss

Most men do not dislodge her
without some show trial
in terms of simple location
nomadism is a place of its own
acutest at its vanishing

Thus the snow will fall
while I am somewhere
listening to a cantata like so little
dark falling out of place
with the rest of wild being

Or asleep in copper beeches
reduced to map the nether way
of detail so easily disowned
inscribed with acids
as the guarantor of the sky above

You call it psychology
a bit eager for a taste of words
again scampering about the attic
a slice of scumbled dreamwork
to complete my meaning

Did you ever think of one thing?
What is your own language?
Another glass in the silvery light
alternating in function between
funk and fiction, go on say it

Most of the time is at stake
for once between the lines of force
something blue branches out
when the phrase returns
singing loudly in both keys

Must we mourn what we say
the mother asks too little
the girl turns to her father his
consulting injury you will think
as I do is a reproach to light

In your writings refrain from
the organic world with one more train
of thought and threaten its taming
not a telepathic message but
the outcome would remain the same

How can we bring this penis
to the fire? or cash the panic
scorn food too much in Italian
verse forms braided tressed and
underwritten in this very room

Believe me the wild place-name
is held to account for me
atop black days for the index
curls up in the cold dreams
with further precipitation in sight

Her screen image only survives
in his sleeping arm my wood
is polished wood and gleams
by the nesting-box of a long
translation from the other past

It is moving what I write
against the odds the heart
of the wheel unties the line
like a wake for a vast conjecture
on the natural production of concepts

Parts of sleep when all is said
and done suggests much more
by the disclosure by an
intervention murmurs in the ear
what is actually perceived

If the far paradigm set fair
in the literal sense of
which he walks over the field
the small sound of wound
must entail a pair of authors

A filial snow against the
fence covers the ends of
lines in unspeakable notation
hard and fast rules at last
in a search for content

Thus the final stage is what
should fill its worst extreme
inner being from this inconstant
of the inner to a language
often speaking at the same time

# from TIME TO GET HERE

POEMS 1969-2002

*Salt*, 2003

## *Poem*

to take up a position as
part of the space you perceive
          turn your back there is
infinite unconscious where I used
to be standing. into which you might
(if an unwary step back)
from the window, fall. with a rain
slipping sidewise in under your eyelids
sad russell street sloping right away
upwards
          a tenure in earth
beside indifferent trees numerous puddles
A rusty wheelbarrow the disordered remnants
of a childhood & one wellington boot
     the sky wd not be any sort
of plane surface nor a single depth
no, full of its own angular exteriority
'a triumph of advanced geometry' & partly
made of brick, and is how you would see us
               even if only
               momentarily

## *The Elegy for Spring*

We have then no mark but
this damp smell which has
enlisted the daffodils the tulips
the wallflowers & the grass
the chestnut trees under
stonework. the guardians of peace
beautiful as a hundred horsemen
dance about the salad/ their red capes.
Have they heard of the Tragedy?
they show no signs of admitting
but "OH! see the arch of the roof
the anger of the butterflies
the knees of the young girls!
dive to them, they are small down there
& your hunger surpasses the sunlight
for merely the look of them ... "
the sky is scarlet &
palpitates at our feet:
the systole is a deceptively gentle action
and as I burn I suddenly realise
being illusory & transitory it is
As interestingly as it began
the music stops. the meadows
float empty &
                                        Is that what the song of the eagles meant?
that these massive caves with
their brick arches are becoming
too hot: I shall get myself
another place to live, where
it will not be you?

## *Kara Chach*

### I

unwithered and gloriously thin-fingered, she is wrapped completely
encompassing horizon the park the street down to the river, hoping
what will happen tomorrow. She jumps into the air crinkling
slightly at the edges of choice (' until the day stone cut scissors')
who is after all not heroic, about to be beset with years of it, he
had to eat it. The door opens slowly
and putting down my fork to begin the journey.
Well, Dr. Wolfgang, has the hidden? we are still wondering
the flat river the liberty to watch them at war or otherwise, what
        have you to tell us?
How believable this scenery is/ 'The past, the sensations of the past!'
but this is only an excuse for something sandier, nearer to love.
How believable this scenery is/ 'The past, the sensations of the past!'
but this is only an excuse for something sandier, nearer to love.

## II

Washing up noises from downstairs light again piles of books round the
bed as usual I'm back again and it's Sunday. The problem of bookshelves
is still unresolved so I resolve to buy some wood tomorrow get things sorted
out I seem to have been using up an awful lot of distance lately like
travelling underground or anyway in a different kind of space though still
quite credible even attractive if you discount the fear the flat river
elms and sycamores glowing across permitted possibilities I traverse in
gumboots nightly. I mean Dragons, really, and the water rising maliciously
over the edge of the sink washing us out into this strange country with
nothing but lumpy earth and me dying of heartfailure gesturing delicately in
the hope of two doves; heroism? it's not even useful, I must get down to some-
thing useful, in fact the only known legacy that has come down to us there
is a common denominator in these ideas. Noises from downstairs again it's getting
darker already the screwdriver is too small the knots keep coming undone the
sauce won't thicken I seem to have been using up an awful lot of time lately
like travelling and dreaming about death and buses the past the sensations of
the past, Dr. Wolfgang has turned into an icon, I think I'll go and talk to Nick.

## *Quiet Arriving*

It would certainly be best if we only counted to sixteen
this time. Remember they said blood was 'a splintery trap
as biological as they come'? well, with a careful titration
it can also help you puff achievement right out
into the freewheeling state
exactly as described on the back of the packet. So
switch off the engine—time to be up and doing, because
we're all off to the everglades.
                                        Yes, she was listening. Her face
shines like an expectation fugue as a golden bird
swoops us up.
Everything is silent
and the swamps give way to the ocean
where a particular green becomes the order of the day.
Occasionally even the shadow of a gigantic seagull
is emblazoned across us, making dilutive forays into
penny-a-hundred disappointments. It's so easy to ignore!
                                        Coming this way, we've avoided
battles and stolen a march on dozens of computer firms.
Lunchtime has mercifully become a thing of the past, all the
surrounding ringlets of lips absorbed, each into its own miniature
range of delights-and all this we are encouraged to call Friend
without the encumbrance of a legacy.
                                        The wording shifts colour momently
here; blood on the grass blades slides liquidly off
while we touch ground where trust
is the whole fleet of our words, and even past it.

# *Summing It Up One of These Days*

When you've been up all night for years
laying bare each vein
and yet the whole physiology
fades to dissolute marble,
does it hurt more than
Would you mind removing your hat?

*Tableau*
The ancient Carolina has been
repainted in purple, and
here it comes, like an iron will o' the wisp
scrunching a bit
like an earthquake in a bunch of violets
then silence

Follow it. Plangently dance the bicycle
to the end of the world.

Ahl Flutes and buskins
all swallowed up now,
remember those times?
after supper on the verandah
and Saturday afternoons in the Boccherini Loggia
dreamily picking at his arms with a pair of scissors...

Oh, toot-toot, the vision is upon us.

the same music clasps
the fields to itself, singing
"When you've a lizard in your pocket, love
whispers politely of the perfect signature."

# *A Happy New Year*

All a-corking in velvet coherence, it's
harder than it looks to leap from 1873 to the postbox but
we do try, and it's so elegant & smells, mmm . . . , familiar.
            All the seventy guns (or such) are out of action;
biding time: *he's* hung up his school cap for good,
determined to cut a figure in the world. Well,
      thin ice these January days.
I don't believe in it myself: flowers occurring near
the drawn-out boundaries of each marshy sentence. Still,
live there until the time comes, eh?
                                                    Perhaps it was condescending
of them to implicate me—they all sail so close under
the meniscus of hope
                                        the slightest touch would be Bungle.
Another thing, whose consideration is at the root of this?
Local days to manipulate, hours of syrtic conversation, we're
all like policemen footing it through yards of treacle.
    Oh, we sail on, affecting nonchalant unconcern
that each meal contains its own version of the last one:
yesterday's recipe was about fudge. Just a few fracid moments
between the years, then suddenly it's all fallen away.
                                             A kitchen landscape you entered
                                             another black telephone to pick up and
you considered my voice as it were an
embryo pearl to be picked up among the grass; in
itself your own heart discarding alternative tints
to come down fair and square in favour of dawn green.
What was that gesture again? Really?

## *Waking Up: 2.10 pm*

The ground is white, four
walls of the courtyard are white,
the white sky is white
                                        Only
          the balls on the white croquet lawn
                    over there
are blue,
          hier in Deutschland.

## *Politics*

the sinking disc inside my eyeball
is solacing itself with gorgeous amber dregs
and the crumbs from a penguin biscuit
scatter like little rabbits I shoot with my teeth

daft Corsican. A patchwork figurine
bobbing in blue water
writing long letters home to be sent in bottles
and tickle the undersides of girls
who swim too far out
and will probably not deliver them.

pull out the thud of hatchets
if you want to be a man.

there are weeds at the bottom of my glass
and my spine is crashing

Marigold, Marigold
are you a freedom fighter?
do you come childless from Bangla Desh?
did you arrive by bus or
were you driven from your country
by an unconditional matter of tattered stucco?

## *Night Ministry*

l glow like a berry
fire about my head
night putting a
porcelain white
seal on the grass

the mouth
nibbles a pudding
and the teeth
snarl enlarged in
the sponge

the nostril
splendid
as grapes
suspended over
me

woolly
fleecy as wool
field of the brain
fire about the head
smoke between
pricking
the eyes

# *Lullaby*

She sleeps for health in terraced cities
banding out note after note evenly
pacifying the tin flies and the sundials
she is the only honest threader.

if I turned over a scarlet portion
difficult fingering makes it slow
because you smile to find your union
and no doubt to relinquish secrets.

blow the trickled music comfortably
and let me hurl accomplishment the wheel
until pins foregather like the hyades
the sweeping monitors of graft.

## *Ritual Slips*

Increase the strong allowances at Easter
and watch it burn, the wood you only love
as flames that twist under neatness all the size

Having each acratic shade of blue
smearcd on my temples made me a dreamer
and 1 buckled on my picnic

Never encountering the piano's rigour
where the sand finished the shrimps up
in what was portraiture of ivories

He started wrong: the haste it took
was planted early and the jug beside his foot
a bleak survey in and out of buckets

A curving hedge to grow from it
that stood as gristle to the next question
the nesting whitethroat's lamp

Believing lunch was ready on the handle
I meant you. Who feathers your lip?
that have planted this herb of incipient violet.

## *Polly Fortune*

it's a late basket underneath
the bottled aspect of the rhododendrons

my sword taints each hand I lay
to the quillon this evening

over the bridge her treading
is to each speedwell like a mottled egg

through the factory wall
another square where the French drink

my shoes have grown up aslant
& bent the grass

## *Red Breath*

you flop to me tonight
when the clutttered table floats
over the bass line in these small hours

you increase like volume
and water me from your padded skull

you turn coracles of scaly wonder
as your legs steady up
into my fat larder

what pain there was
you fly it like a flagman
busy with the red fern

and you reach for the starver
in king needles of even breath.

## *Hold the Child Father Sunlight*

The new months are blown until
the Kent coast sharpens where we file
it into our returning eye

spiced up into a colder light
to marching yellow faces
a sea full of terns for a socket

I persuaded some to liberty among
nettles for tickets to your proud teeth:
Hold the child, father sunlight, to the greater canvas

while the instant of colour stays
where we were, mud-crowned to the nines,
and knew the way and the blue expanse.

# *Sparkling Fruit Salts*

## Kino

Never be alone. Cell
protein constructs its
narrative in the dark
& we sit taking in aerial
snaps of receptor sites
proper conditions of
sense whirring across
the surface of the reel
crime & every mounting
sentence resounds
appealing and falls flat
against the screen where
there is no conversation
blinding growth first
egg of history
flickers and proposes
a resolution of some
more celestial device

## Lino

*for Denis Roche*

No admittance board gleamed above hedges
or nests of pippit rejoined the lost
cuckoo of summer, opening eyes in early sun-
light as re-entry into the forbidden
matter of dreams
such a future is inconceivable
amulet of tender stance useless against
my power of hatred and its speckled
vision collimated or transcribed for two
flutes and a barrel-organ. Buff
architecture like in Florence lacks the
lyric presence of granite. I wonder if
song is a mineral function of our material
chemistry crystallising the substance of
each ideational trace of our passing?

# Nino

co-workers refuse offers of dis
junction appropriate to a landscape
of pineal variety more than the board
room where I thought your shape improper
your smartly groomed pubic hair verged
on the blasé veered off
that moment's utterance into buttercup
fields of your arse as memory
my linguistic referents laze in
polymorphous undergrowth scatt
ered in a corner of my research
casamatta where I escape floods and
bombs and the thud thud of pine
cones fruitless occasions the surf
torn jacket shifting beneath the surf
ace of a role she might see as im
personal amid miscellaneous visions
mirrors confronting an innocent
subject with its constant
business of living

## Rhino

eye this tragedy of
unmasked circumstance pink
faces reveal trembling leaves
something to seize
hold on to removed
from actual life
would you allow me
an encyclopaedia a neigh
bouring bed in the
munitions plant
ation? Quick hide geranium
seed floating formally
acquitted but still
guilty oral or not to
carry your house on your
foolish back grind
your horn the pool of
reminiscence I regard
as my amorous history
we inhabit as
ground it all thunders
with its approach

## Vino

Effractive light falls
on her from its
source behind the lens
breaks and simply pours
glass after glass
enough to limit
pressure on the round
fruit rinsed of cog
nition in such baths
of what seems like
pure planes of what
I always thought
I ever knew
Would contain it all.

## *The Yurt: Day One*

### 1. THAT THE PERSONAL QUALITIES HE HAD GAINED IN THIS WAY BELONGED

From the cities. From other places. Twelve arrived for the three days.

"An *aitys* demanded great resourcefulness and, most off all, an ability to improvise." The choice includes abuse, panegyric, mockery and exchanges (contests) of wisdom and knowledge. I excluded, as degenerate, competitive collective form work.

The yurt was rapidly assembled, metal and skin among others, mind interface. A tent of thought for mutual habitation and pleasure. "that those poets whose mental level does permit them to / know order". The weather is always important.

### 2. BY VIRTUE OF ITS LIMITATIONS, IN OTHER WORDS BY VIRTUE OF A

"But far more mightily than by the past is the mind influenced by the future; the former leaves behind only the quiet perceptions of remembrance, while the latter stands before us with all the terrors of hell..." (Feuerbach). All those who wanted to live in another world, the situational architecture of the yurt, the moment of grazing, came hesitant and more or less cynical to the place, on the grounds that they were going in that direction anyway. So much for intense local seriousness, local is caused by social time. Our mouths opened in uncertain speech, advent of hope ("many of the events referred to under the catch-all term 'tone of voice'") walked, skinned up, had a drink.

## 3. THE WAR WAS IN THE LAST EVENT AN ANTICLIMAX

Everybody retired to Berne library to read *The Science of Logic*. Art. Nick said he didn't think much of *High Pink on Chrome*. (None of the Old Ones were at the vurt, although Mike Haslam found some footprints near the stream, We were deeply concerned over their presence in the yurt's fabric in case there was a storm.) I argued staying at home. risking the very simplest food, entering the field through elevated rehearsals of the music of paraconceptual possibilities unavailable to the ordinary neurologist. In five dimensional space, the music of the spheres demands an improvisatory topology. the internal surface of the world, the roof of the yurt.

## 4. OBLIGATIONS OF HIS OWN CONFIRMED HIS FEELING

"that the Mind or Will always

successfully opposes & invades the Previous"

It was an argument that began. The set text was *Lud Heat*, nobody knew whether lain Sinclair would arrive, whether he had already been translated or if he was there like the missing things hidden somewhere in the picture. Si tu penses pour les autres, ils penseront pour toi. For this session the yurt was urban, and nothing changed. Martin accepted the 'danger of metal finish', I wanted to talk about Tatlin's dream.

The frame of our temporary world expanded, its central geometry became clear to all. But it was only a sign.

## 5. ON ONE'S CHEEKS

Schwitters's imagazine *Pin* never got off the ground. It was intended to be the hole people had to creep through to see what art is all about. We all agreed to oppose creeping. I am introducing this to you. It is not my place to offer homage. I wear a beard, which I keep short. Next to arrive were Nigel Wheale and John Seed:

"the human eye, when, inside it does not know
any more than what it can express by living &
that sight be in this man's eye is the expression we call love:"

## 6. HALF OF ALL HUMAN ASSERTIONS SIMPLY CANNOT BE TAKEN SERIOUSLY

What's more, I must explain that these chapter headings are taken, by means of a random number sequence provided by Deborah, from Volume 1 of *The Man Without Qualities*, which was also chosen randomly, and were not discussed at any stage during the yurt itself.

## 7. FIGHT

a possible explanation of our joint presence was proposed by this heading. We reject it for its connotations of violence without hurt. We formed a circle facing outwards and chanted "a dream is constructed by the whole mass of dream thoughts being submitted to a sort of manipulative process in which those elements which have the most numerous and strongest supports acquire the right of entry into the dream content", while inhibitory theories of cortical activity circled around.

## 8. DOWN WAS NOTHING COMPARED TO THE REALITY

lan reported on his visit to the lan Tyson exhibition at the Tate, where in order to see the prints he had had to clamber round people eating lunch. Four people had moved their meals to other tables or other parts of the same table, one had complained loudly. and another had had his coffee spilt by the viewer as he stepped back suddenly from 'field of blood, sound of wave'.

## 9. AMONG THE FEW MEN WHO HAD AN INFLU-

Peter Philpott introduced the session on the search for pleasure. He began by quoting Einstein: "Behind these essays lies above all an epistemological requirement which derives from the gestalt psychological point of view: beware of trying to understand the whole by arbitrary isolation of the separate components or by forced or hazy abstractions." Martin came in with some words of Engels from *On the Housing Question*: "really being in love means wanting to live in another world [...] The orgasm [...] is a glimpse of a transformed universe." By now it was late afternoon, misty and dusky, and the walks were over.

## 10. THE FOLLOWING PAGES FROM A LETTER

" . . . the decadence of former notions of public presence, idealistic communities, etc., is exposed." Perhaps you would agree, though, that *that* proposition is really based on the idea that they aren't, that functioning, localized energy is more than just the historical path it assumes, takes into itself the rejected idea, is self-defining as continuity rather than revolution? Attached to this note is the resolution agreed by seven of the twelve who came to the yurt, on the future of painting. What do you think about point iii?

## 11. SAME ENDLESS FORCE, SWEPT TO LEFT AND RIGHT

I think your readers will probably find that heading self-explanatory. By late evening the yurt was complete, the constructional geometries of Spinoza and Einstein had succeeded in providing complete twelvefold siamese thought shelter. (cf esp. *Ethics*, Part III Prop LV, Note 1.) We sat in silence and prepared Day Two and Day Three.

## 12. HAD HAPPENED FOR THE FIRST TIME HOW HIGH THE SKY REALLY WAS

## *The Audience*

The audience for a poem is silence. Listening
awakes somewhere inside you, and the language
spreads out till it has claimed your entire skeleton
and filled with its presence the volume your skin encloses

You don't absorb it. Like when some biologist injects
a blue dye into some small translucent organism
it's not absored. You become a perfectly controlled
airship, and sail into action like a musical phrase.

## *'Life Dreamed Now Life Lived' (David Gascoyne)*

black on white
the first up on the wall turned back
their glowing eyes
our thousands of feet
on the ground

what woke me this morning
in the middle of the bed
puffy clouds sailed past the window

the pylons on the hill
stretched like a stocking before
it's pulled over a face

a black stocking
on a white face

such clean straight lines
they might have come from you
and our blob oforange

## *Derry*

these gardens sharp and previously unextended
sense of the possible prints on the wet grass
wasted evenings completed by some arabesque
of guns and cameras and turning film waiting to
go home piled injustice burning outside the flats
and the shapes it all takes look rather like us

## *The Political Economy of Art*

You will see the good housewife
taking pride in her
pretty tablecloth,
and her glittering shelves,
no less than
in her well-dressed dish,
and in her full storeroom;
the care
in her ocuntenance
will alternate with gaiety,
and though you will reverence her
in her seriousness,
you will know her
best by her smile.

## *Underground*

*for Peter Ackroyd*

here's your address
it glows apprehensively
& undertakes a relaxation of personal work
up in the sun
where the act of striking breaks hearts...
the bicycle is binding too
loves to hear you sing
as maps unfold the summer
we call out hopefully as if the tune was dead
only axles clutter the yard
like fieldfares later on.

I tell you how I feel
over something to drink in Southwark
and watch your expression contract;
the first results came up on the screen
those drunken wires
grassing it out in other coppices
and beside reservoirs in the pennines:
here's your economy, bone by bone,
& I shall not stop undermining
these children of europe or book you as
the season's distraction
look there's the drop now
I know you'll confront it.

## *Looking at Henry*

Our unavoidable fate        not the Surrealists, the door
  deeming energy our purity nasquerade.
                    Pearls hover, the last post
      is flattery
        and the path of the militia in winter
  lost under the snowfall
from a neck:
                  no question of force
              of will, or writer's cramp.
The bends of space and time *is* not,
  it *happens*
                  without distance in light;
so much for defiance-
*Nothing will ever stop people meeting each other's eyes*

  That's safe, an assertion from above, and
none the less true for that.
Conquest. A condition
              of perfectly neutral word
            that already exists in the block.
It makes no difference to Henry, owning the dream,
        dreaming it from wall to wall,
                    if he eats the eye
                    like a stocking before it's pulled over a face.
Just a peak of actual surfaces, your crystal-clear intentions
          and his moral imagination
                    together between the covers
a single impulse of inept combination.

## *Sestina*

Autumn as chill as rising water laps
and files us away under former stuff
thinly disguised and thrown up on a screen;
one turn of the key lifts a brass tumbler—
another disaster probably averted, just,
while the cadence drifts in dark and old.

Voices of authority are burning an old
car on the cobbles, hands on their laps,
as if there was a life where just
men slept and didn't strut their stuff
on stage. I reach out for the tumbler
and pour half a pint behind the screen.

The whole body is in pieces. Screen
memories are not always as sharp as old
noir phenomena. The child is like a tumbler
doing backflips out of mothers' laps
into all that dark sexual stuff
permanently hurt that nothing is just.

I'm telling you this just
because I dream of watching you behind a screen
taking your clothes off for me: the stuff
of dreams, of course. Tell me the old, old
story, real and forgetful. Time simply laps
us up, like milk from a broken tumbler.

A silent figure on the stage, the tumbler
stands, leaps and twists. He's just
a figure of speech that won't collapse
like the march of time and the silver screen;
like Max Wall finally revealing he was old
and then starting again in that Beckett stuff.

I'd like to take my sense of the real and stuff
it. There's a kind of pigeon called a tumbler
that turns over backwards as it flies, old
and having fun; sometimes I think that's just
what I want to do, but I can't cut or screen
out the lucid drift of memory that laps

my brittle attention just off-screen
away from the comfortable laps and the velvety stuff
I spilled a tumbler of milk over before I was old.

## *New York*

Touched by a lifetime
response left like a cloud
in her eye as yet buried

last nunmber recall buttons
tendered and the connection
doesn't want to pay for

what you know anyway
she is smiling on the subway
in about 1958, at night

called a sheaf of young writers
quasi una shadow crossed
precisely at three thirty

marked by writing perhaps
until it was finished, and even then.

## *Oh Snooty*

*for Ben Watson*

Off the bone we swing down the street
heroic old figures full of stillness in
face of listless farewells and inky tropes
for thinking over. The cold blue sky is free
of smudges even if not simultaneously gassy
enough to breathe openly, caught at the
moment of birth in a circling whoosh of
extended caprice like molecules of national
emergence into a betrayal of all we once stood
for. Carry this for me while I count wave
after wave of sorry explanation, coming back
first class with stars in his eyes from an evening
of tacky piano fumblings and savage policy.
When I was younger I read the passage transcribed
above, and lost confidence in land, handed
back and put together with pipe-smoke point
of view about contracting pupils and mournful
time over the summer. It could equally well be
so now, if some version of it was playing
locally, quietly, round the corner. Between paintings
there is this wash deeper in brilliance
and may be already gone when you put it down
as his grief. A problem has happened
has been dedicated as I ask now at the end of
demanding more lifetime correspondence of our
health and our work. And indeed there was a job for him
although he kept on writing. The windows broke
and the army displays a genuine soul business
with bombs and rockets and madness and romance
like a stage advantage conscious of huge details
of a small lampshade which is present and mad enough

in a torture chamber coming round all the time
about to change back into song clatter.
Much more to grind is also the main individual
thing, in the comfort of his own guilt. In violence
on the new statute we replay the fifties among
the glasses, the dishes, the sofa, the story's remorse.
Don't elide the words, they mean everything to you.

# *Oh, To Be in England*

What is this state if affection binds to shatter its
own suturing, if empty light throws up damages,
if stuttering vehicles pose as derivative maxims and admonitory
puzzles of blind restraint? How smart can these be?
The wooden surface belies substance, the soft cloth of
years deepening gloss to a pitch of narcissism
fluted bravely to clinging air. Catch it before it goes
too far, please deflect the ice topics, dead looks
bound by both types to deserve a figurative cool benevolence.
Oriental grounds leech the final vision for padding steps
down to two earlier pages, to form a cortical sale
eager to grow a second skin. She let fall a kind of remark. A spine
of no human place combining blue with whiter skin
failed to juggle with them in the dark fashions of conjugation,
attacked the children in a crowd of syrupy poisoners
bursting through the door for the sober results of an obscure fear.
Shock in its crudest liturgy would form a crust
on the pool surface, ringing and ringing through the quiet gardens,
to live more difficult passages to our line, as in the case
of death's soft clothing. What are these very dark things
growing in a pot? The most acute dots are memories
done with a pin or the point of scissors, facing the light of day
to a point on the ego. Only one barrier, of not harming,
has fallen upon the child with teeth. It's a working model
in our sleep, the imprint of a hand that was changed into a prophecy.
If this can only be a system, the water will close over its state,
with a creased photograph floating on it like ice.

## *Pastoral*

By splicing information
that causes luminescence
in deep-sea fish
into grass seed,
Californian biotechnology
is catching up
with poetry.

But it is used
to enhance
domestic security:
& nobody dances
by lawn light.

## *After Pope*

*for Lisa Robertson*

The bust pressure of a broken pottery ear
Must fail for a singing glitz graphology, but
Dial a breath anyway my receptor
Is silvering. In the human ledger
The liripipe is a new-found room to think
Who's atop the drive. Holding your force to my dial
Does not insist on holding your vase to my
Prior writing. When I bleed we all eat
The word pasture, have to do it—auguries
Aside—(literally) a real assignment.
Anyway I sigh manfully for actions attuning
To the renown arena. An inner renown arena musty
With seed of a wise expenditure of telepathy? I might
Goad a thinker or advocate a bottle of soda or do
What I think I forced in magic and then ate anew, lighting the longing
For failing. Light the shores of falling
For your row boat against stopframe forest
King Love Queen Love—what a word—till my whole
Aspen trails over bubbling waters and I'm a
Bloke and a pen originally afraid of a
Last flumy tendance. Fuck. Even my dear
Morbid quiddity's in flush camelot. Slow me now
Unspeakable oval and its consort pen
As a silly voice wails write the poem.
Please. Steal me some poetic tide, an untapped
Harvest halo to mark a human reflex,
A bullet in the heart. This very thing perceives
Each lighted stubble, stumbles, slumber
Wakes her pillows: away with the silvering in
My receptor! we are unfrocked as
Privates in the reactional republic

Of the poem's toil and in some way dissonantly
Wasting and waiting on steps still hands
Always missing a planted foreboding lungs
On the tip of the tongue. till hands always
Wrestling with flickers of gorgeous trauma
Win nothing but this button I carry
As we die

## *Laugh Like a Piano*

*after T. S. Eliot*

Stunned under hotspur vehemence, odd
starlings on a garden gnome,
we waver, descend lightly yonder
glass-pure flows, your withers panting apace,
& fall then to the ground in turn
with a few gipsy mementos in your ice
bottles waving twice to some light in the air.

So a wood has hidden leaves,
So a wood has adders tanned and angry,
So a wood has letters
solely vested & boding dawn ambrosial,
as the mined desert forebodes hazard.
Ice defined
as a wave incompatible with life and death,
as a way with a boastful ampersand
& an implant faceless as a mile shaking the sand.

Sheets torn away bitter as the external weather
impaled my margin, harsh Eumenides.
Money, descend O Money! How is
a hero ever harmed in sandals, arms feeling so loose
as I wander home that they shoot a bond trader.
My shirt has lost a chest, your hand a posy.
Some tunes these cozy stations steal amuse
The rubble. Midnight. And no-one's repossessed.

## *Basic White*

*after Geoff Ward*

If in the night a voice is heard
crying out in awkward passages to
confirm characters' hidden wishes,
or the struggle with time becomes buried
in the volume of utterance like snow so as
to resemble the fan of cards in a refusal
to face indulgence and strive to exist
in that regard almost fragile and fictive—
a step away from the grave passage as a trap
for the unwary casts judgment on the first
unity of politics or might have preferred
to be adept at the slender space
lamenting (as some do) direct statements
and the most compendious abandonment.
Yet we need not believe him as the figures of fogbound
signification in basic white pains and still want
surprisingly candid echoes of a serious hope
already at work within the margins.
An exercise in light may still be
a meditation on the death of a band
posing as the textual snow of a thick story
of speech, lies, and such conceits
alongside the desire of a child for the ultimate
blood built out of words like a thirst already
at work within the weapons that outstare me.

## *Hardihood*

**1**

Change sun by sun and fling and laugh
as any spot that now had fired the waste
from the bill twitted within my brain's
winter edge, shaped in slow regret.

I wrote two letters. Given words to mine
it cuts like my table carried off by name:
touchdown will carry you back unpaid
as a vane would disjoint witchery from me.

This can of shapes from the files is a spot
when he'll come equal into the streets,
as we did with a more crashing iron fire,
a little string and a working flare pane, maybe.

Flung my iron to the bushes, to the stair.
before a cupboard. Our hands, her personal
arch stood in homespun reason's blink
burst by numbers and without the walls.

Cornered or vast, what was this green grain
to the wild eye in a ferny ring,
broached to turn with self to thin sense
between yours and mine, the sun's lip upcast?

Even no sign under her pin, steel and stone
vanished and returned on the panel.
The names had failed where the mist felt the dust,
phantom hints gone for response to open.

The name changing the barren tree
to shades of irony, rapt in the true one
to her ruin from bee slumber. Mile by mile
I come to my voice, the grasp of other.

I was like a tract on every side
as I stood in a rose spot where even the new reasoning
looked radiant, breathed all our lives
in mothy walls, under archways of thought.

Now as early measure forbids writing
I conceive laughter and a light green breath
set in unrest and small ash trees. My page
is in my space, my light like silent zest.

I claim to feel I cannot find my lack
in bespoke ends, flush within that day
your body gazed and gazed far up my stair
boring within my bones, and moved things.

Drain the light wasted by sleeves in risk,
give space stairs in secret. Nettles in your bread
the incipient lines do indeed say green
by this and skin my cold equanimity.

## 2

Pronounced or heard, hid here in the late spring
while red shapes of puppets circle
and rust, I'm apt to lift you back, loving as rain.

Scarce guns in their yellow kiss stood
under the arch called circumstance
yet at that time no rent was set to the years.

Rest breaks strange stars in the waning cold
of meaning, to be still as wings. Beyond earth's doings
a father broods, speaking at a spot, and on the sky.

Last and stay, cling and greet the sick men
in blue light and dim thought of zest.
Flash out a slit through chrome frippery.

Form lies in a pinch to be ecstatic
till the image raised the plot, blind and blended
with each dome to spell cove and abrade each groin.

In the day shapes sink as ripples out of nothing.
I can recall a man who died by an alley
hurled into the sun by the bloody darkness,

And crushed like a bent tune. Extinct romance
may be silent on its long trace and count as mine,
perplexed in these late tappings and distortions.

I said iron shall perish to a shining black regret
and leave some impulse missed on the eclipse
of immense human war crimes and wounds

To life, and maybe what I believe unlit with replies.
What is worse than unanswered broods in the night
Of laws which attack life, their sleep-worker and song.

## 3

Opened tissues feel
one wild frame from dawn
till we go to speak

Yet she never succeeds
those millions of daily messengers:

I say some scheme tore shape
by a word flash through my land

Written on the poor unconscious flesh
that I still traverse through the heat.

## 4

Fear and dwindle waste the ear
No hint to fly to sense:
lgnorant skies shut earth's wide tear
And bide unreasoning yet.

Today organic dust will wane,
Be lit and unfold as this moment
Had just begun to speak
For a red cloud by the home.

When I edged a shape by this
I broke my word and left off
Biting these cheeks and bonded
With a broken time that knew it.

Between now and a guarded tongue
My face is froth, not fate:
I need to find things I knew,
A spot by no trace of old intent.

Meet me at my tread with preoccupation,
Which grew as the call for hours;
Follow my scared dead seasons
Into a thin sound screened from the eye, swallowing things.

## 5

In the patient world, be an instant
It subdues. Times drop their fires
And we think we drop a blind moth.
My page in space the lamp.

Know how days are birds turned to men:
Birds used to feed us shapes that cry in frost
Till delay took the shine in a mask
And the eye of strings trembled through air.

We swim on form and stony hands
As the door to less and the scarce steps:
Content is gone to name his fancy protest
Where feet mounted the will with his cameo.

Her thoughts track the sun to the lawn end
In rooms by now happier than winter:
The vent of pain is familiar, her dry ears
Wrenched to a text we half ruined.

This could have been bewitched by feathers
If thought did not cut masks with a pencil.
See that poetic water? Banks change shape best
As I look at knowledge, not you in spring.

All alight with bitter fields, the blind
Find my messenger breath gleaming red and cold
In the twigs, prone to a hurried request
To one who wrote back these eyes.

No feet bestow me where you walk beside sight,
The door emblazoned twice in the frost:
Black is best and dust has no shapes—
Matter is delight and fear, shaped in my path.

## 6

*for Jenny*

The stolen world, glowing and benighted with vision,
Ending over my ivoried task, moves and burns;
So now I draw this spot to that field in the dark
And calm all the stone time of my words.

And now the nettle did blow. It wears my fate.
I trace feet from shapes that dance
Through the night for little cost,
And shade her eyes with no repayment, no calm.

I scanned each lost child for time at his pause,
And dwindled to be left like his name:
Memory is a crumbled tree, a spectre in a mind
That may be wrong as in song the peewits grieve.

Now a rose and an arid silence heat my presence
Against the green skyline. She thought that voice spoke
Of my father, between dream and content,
Full of steep surprise, its curve wasted by sunlight.

Then the form of time did not return again?
Fifty years faced the dry tap and I heard Johnny's tale
In time to the wind as light dispersed the files,
And the plans I once had approached the tract of words.

The first voice was dead. I wondered what secret door
Went out through the fields beyond me. Can my mouth
Close while words lie within me? I sang the tune
We sang walking in the summer when form is fire.

## 7

*for Jenny, again (Happy Birthday)*

After all the breath, we were altered of heart
And at last each circumstance was mine,
The yew line to her every story consigned
To new lines and conventions within her precincts.

Spells of time may account for unregarded sea,
And then more times in the street,
In that long winter breath in the memory
Before names step in to my eyes and speech.

Dancing as we lay and moved like sparks
Of living ashes in a bower of breath,
I passed my heart and changed, smiling
More eyes with nothing beyond two.

What array of speech did they cover
Outside Paradise on the windows between!
Distance was a spot under the dark show
And will repeat your name through and through.

But O you, presence that fingers a close time
At dawn in sudden lines that die like a cloud,
The kind eyes, the thought with all it cannot blank,
Reached us sleeping, body and soul resumed.

## 8

You need no door with me, never the manifold tints
in some fancy life after a dead past. You are the spots
in a voice just the same as our note and the pale waves.

We burst in wild junction and slowed to something fled.
Time has been unflinching as rain says what a day thinks
just after noon in the mind and its phantom turns.

As a vision touches thought and, yes, bears eyes
that slip on jade to the door, to the dwelling where fire blows
and the sea pieces this finger, I still stand under the rooks.

You gaze from news of glass and smile about it between
my dim eyes wrapt in filmy time. Shift things from the table
and persist in words for circles and presences that see me.

Having said this. a trace of word paused before a splash
of dawn parted the horizon of things menaced by need
and its coppery march, till all was warm air and suspended here.

## 9

Who thought about her old poet and his discredited comrade?
My social ghost thought something I owned without clinging
to the gift like rain would wake me like a web from a wall.

That stone in the hall shone by his syllables. Obliterate my song
to-morrow. I forget dreaming for phantoms want it and still
the uncaring light will sing insects in the mind, peacefully.

No one touch the dazed breath on the roof with voices till my whim
let him ride down the long grave, wings turning in from the door.
The moon rose through the crack in light, a mirror of its shadow.

I forgot the window, emerging into the empire left by memory,
the spot of polished oak right on my intellect as if off my finger
my blustering crowd slid in small white threads with eyes revolved.

A whim can fail. Step behind this spot and a page appears, retained
in her mind this time like blankness. The poet has to pause till
her glance pervades his cover, and they must sit and smoke.

You see you put your choice on the edge of my hand. And the air
will pass daily into my arms and not perceive me. My time's burning
late, you marvel, and your eyes catch the voice in things, again.

## 10

Why should breezes glow more than my own window
Silken waste, elms like trees there as a break
in a space of the universe when I call you up, and mavhe
the word made the past an alley feather.

Sight will be my image on the eye, visible words
only being sound breathed at each face in the line
Against each look back I nail a certain moon
as soon as the posts come to my pencil in dreams.

On like the breath, always to recall like a bright guest,
I went into the look of choice, into my ear, rushing down
to nearer to here. Between lines and no shape I heard
all this, groping after that wire bird in its voice.

By these eyes, my page was aware, my vision a shining
tragedy in string and screens anyhow. Washed with soot,
I paid for things I warned my darling of, and the figure
of the trees rises in the white voice from the leaves.

Will you take dust as a phantom mistake by the day?
This mist in me in the night was a book I made, a twist
of the drift written on my own eyes when I put it back
as the yellow space called the cloud ended in air.

## 11

I looked under a figure that declined a trace of afternoon
like string. like a song above new frosts and the dread coffin
on that spot far from the brothers. Ordinary thought at last.

I used to damp the light when the photograph gnawed my eyes
but the card was lost and the deed was casual. I could shape
distance like a path of white stones cut in a glass.

O here are nerves and black night, and a phantom earth!
A figure is always to be desired where the pencil knows
that irony of utter rhyme, my strange memory of stone and finger.

I regard others between us as the breeze, red as your day
in February, as fog hung in the eye, fog like vision in its hat
with me in the curves of things behind my back less shadowed.

In the porch I watched smartly while the household died. Old
mothers with hands frame the same moth, as if red goes away
in thought and she was coming with wings to drop down on a lawn.

It's not my foot, it's the skeleton of naked wires standing in the dust
red and slow that placed it in the string like a sanguine livery
and detached the fallen fingers we know still travel from her arms.

I go from my screen, from the quick waves and the white clocks,
seeing things and missing you as well as the air from eyes
in the grass, never looking across to the phantom outside the image.

## 12

When her image shone upon the glimpse, the core in sight
of the Muses would rise into the night. The next room
breathes as if it saw a red scarf and blind string fill it
till my wonder looked up and knew they spoke to me.

This has happened. At times I follow by the sea as a screen
for bared lives, tugged by eyes in the poise of one in the morning.
The hard sky looked over me, a bee in the sun was the mark
over my shoulder, mine to last like a vision of two pieces.

What she did, where it means nothing behind grief, I wrote
on the nettles miles from the railway. I printed the book
with casual words in the dark clock you can hear each day.
my dear, like a mood in a mask of the words I believe.

A hazed voice under the clouds would burn in the frame.
next to some doorstep, as thought prints the same things
round your bites. Ask why we called before. It was the neck.
Between the stone and my shoulders the fall of a leaf went on.

I wanted to go home, my treasure, and stand
and think in your frame just to see this face. Perhaps we
had better wish that any tune held the figure you said was dumb
and rambling, almost forgotten in flesh like living eyes.

The eye may not see the dust. I breathe your bread, hoist
my gear from railtrack and put on a story of the author.
When night comes I borrow the robe by the door,
come to my love and listen in the dark to my name.

## 13

Who said gambling made sleep spectral? Who wants to drown
the sun silently without a dusk where creatures rise again?
Outside the rooks rise and fall in his ear, ferns shade the wheels
behind bare time and the dancing clay in words is spectral and uncertain.

To know that the glass behind the dream here is stone, and the dusk
is this wheel outside your gate, was as if my name closed again
in blankness and we saw things dissolving in each line I read
by the poet in you. The doors will hold them in and shape the waste.

I can please nyself like you, but the morning will rumble my vision
of this house. I rush to find the most austere chapter in the dust,
the whitest room you knew, as the air shapes the pale gate again
where an unknown glance moves away in irony from the rest.

## 14

A threaded crowd, tortured beyond fear, walked slowly
apart from where I left my windows open. A form kept on
as if the house heard me try to meet a man in the avenue.
She is a star to follow in the street by my curtains, I sang.

My tongue tried finding my love to stand in the avenue,
and I went out to a place.

## *Quite Right*

Roosting starlings in the pink January dusk
Cluster like thoughts on branches
Outside my door and extend inward in
Vast overlapping trees of mental function.

One or two million of these
Dispositions of being I try to evoke with
This figure: anticipation and cognition are
Just everywhere as the dimensions start to fall

Out of my control like futures. I'd forgotten
The vast and besetting systems of roots
Sustaining each branch they land on, grip

And set in place. In fact, they define it in
New complexity as it gets harder to see out,
And opacity reclaims each brief transparency.

# *A World of Love*

## I

Beginning caused her tonight
her lovely air triumphing.

She beat more to make her silent
then called, 'I expect not.'

She swung away towards eloquence
in step, ice was being made

between two pairs of eyes;
just not doll enough to be a mouthpiece.

In a voice of all people she said Why here,
or indeed in the world at all?"

This is my experienced chiffon
cut hastily, nothing better,

the dress of her body to face
the impervious fortification

## II

To be nothing left now, air or husks
gathered into a peak of languor,

about somewhere here in the room.
Minutes of intense being instead of dancing.

There had been 'writing' only
by reading the optic sequence:

but what was Jane to make of it?
She began to undress partly and partly.

Sensuous hot night, altogether spilled out,
then the word 'obelisk' caught her eye.

## *Death of Dance*

In the world bounds become battered down
to the state. Accidents are on the spot.

Good sense in a taxi
loses its isolated public
its level dread of the universal.

The proper word, the faultless grief,
comes from the taste of people:

You are doomed by seeing in the sky.

## *In the Train*

The slam of a dozen
on the verge of an utterance

mysterious and personal, a piece of hair
made the room sadden him

each time was to clarify everything
but the injury was haunted like a picture

with an eye full of red dusk
I was surprised that he would define relief

Shut his penetrating eye
one moment of failure to consider dead

part of himself, I know, I know,
just for an hour or two.

# *North*

Under conditions where people wept
I stopped the car. Sleep, in fact, like a petal

he wanted simply. His eyes
had no clocks, did not turn round,

had a good head. Somebody
caught the light of justice, pale and puffy,
aggressive and quick.

"But how did you get here?" she said
like spirits at his chambers

and saw the fumy void: possibly no one
in the car. The repose of windows

the tray, the tune like this,
like some ragged and bulky cloud
stood in her overcoat.

He just wants rapid advantage;
thank him. But I think we should be better.

## *Living Here Now*

Down by the first curtain
in the very first line
you seemed not to be denied
fire in a different key

daylight nothing but afternoon
no sign of a newspaper
forming like rivermist
you stood hands in pockets

also there was a picture
between the chair and the sofa
you had your own house
based on your own words

we think about terror
from time to tine
trying to knife the bread
of cataclysm trauma and pride

it was a renewal of difficulty
the west was jagged with flames
then it all died down
and the thin air was full of today

this illusion we name ours
this one iron note in the room
makes you immortal
in the intensifying light

## *Mulch Tumult*

*For Stephen Rodefer*

Munch ado about the light and the get-it-on mensch has captivated
like an electric shock a few people or their words which he keeps
in a jar on a shelf. Captivated, titivated, captured or capsized. If the cap
fits William, lazing on a sunny afternoon, chatting idly in Malay
then wear it, dear Liza, and be called to the bar of Heaven like a lecture
on Aristotle or more likely one on Catullus. Lucretius makes them go
wild, too.
It's a happy birdie to use when the nightingale don't work anymore,
and the last laugh is in yet another language. A handy way to drive
in old company is to take the wheel in a proper glove and just go
for a spin, dark glasses on your nose, turning that wheel of fortune
like a barker. Too much quotation makes you blind, my duck, and allusion
doesn't hit the spot either. It's the waterfall of rhetoric, the torrent of
inventive being in a glass house darkly, listening to the stones. 'We should
really like to see into his head, we do it by pointing to something red,
every sign by itself seems dead.' Meaning something is like my image
of him.
It might deserve the name 'investigation'. Give me your ornate ears, as
Louis said.

# THE GLASS BELL

*Barque Press, 2009*

*Alors au lieu de tout brûler on commence à aimer les fleurs.* (J.D.)

*Daylight and radio waves fade.* (J.D.)

## *I. Glossalgia*

Chose wire direct today for news to see maintained
skies resisted down and more remembered cheer
dispassionately redetermine parts, or particulars,
like authorial ace catches soft rope, pull equal
alabaster summit. Aroma di parma, comma,
enters in lemony flicks. NASA not shamed by ear
two passages tightly pressed, sets of angels, strange sets:

that astringent quest for show to be a graphic
hotel dancer structurally in those days meant to
rest on latex. Lest in nature rest
a too sepia future, ending the first sentence
in a prim lazy tone, machete chased to
a real cottony nude unknowable concept
of The Thing: magnified, classy, elephantine.

Many are dead, UK occasional filth come home to this
hollow this last structure of a poétique France
fear runs abroad wires travelling from the same home on
the list tucked sure of the floor, comma, does the truth part here
formally. Sell to a modern circular or sell a man
or a vin rosé to mouth a tune to tease Sunday roses
ask if he's a saint (as Truman said) all pink and naked:

dove loss cool as clamour cool over here
as gender lacks the knowledge demon under an old fig tree
oh Perdita the very fear swirls out as arugula
more and more drunk on a ciderly familiar pause
violent lays certain petals hourly down paddles in pearly
alocasia knocks apples down pansies down
questioned by another logic day sharpens the garden.

Surly crust of thought brought skinny id to vanity's
apparat. Surly surly is your foe, delight a sky
I know or ponder so, see me pensively expansively
and, comma, the fallout a natural reptile in steel
limit all resemblance to war and dance where
lily flowers panic to shiver cancerous cells
with light on too many soap aid operas looming by:

the bells satiny dash in a merely earning negative
or ashcan spirit intones verse on paper
swings big money in fact-finding sexy policies.
Is this asylum or atonement? Home-made quiche, crumbled cheese
seize the chance of writing down every manky fact
sent here to bend lines down summery prison dells
adjunct adjourned to chew and roll in sidereal distances.

And let masked granaries stand by the same authority
coded to use appropriate force as key to a coming appearance
tried sitting, comma, very antic hay and an instant answer
to ravel chains luminous composure palms the schemata
left on the sticky headline. One law is a line in this sorry bubble
entered as days or justly left out of a firm's future.
Visibility dies as meat foremost in terror. Gold effects *in vitro*:

divide article to show savvy at role methods
(say vole) numinous batons too cool to delete a letter
nor know why a moment came nor fate daintily change
foot (*durch die Verwandlung*) as indeed it did result.
Law lord why do you fantasise such deep lost office?
Twitter on, what's done exists to change the subject,
hit the exit, exiting the stranger's back so lunar and starry.

Two columns incite pages of crusted spoon-feeding
assimilate primal fear as perfect fear, common egg seed
airtex dramas throwing up defensive offers to the language
a snip at 6K a day—because it's the law
with obsequious names, sweet tailoring, like get fucked
is mistraduction or hallucination all over again
always farming between high purple hills and mean:

reception's spire and truncheon ease the wrinkle
of cultures, history issues burn moths in the cloud ways
allsorts tied to mar such lapis fragments as are taken in
also by mouth foaming for a cure while not only guillemots
thicken the air marks march from edge to edge by size
or fall for it sheer tumble from mill to terraces beating
midsummer with Richard Perle lost in the fleeting crowd.

Leaving meant ditches sealing the last rickety nest
single here in the Levant plus total force to dessicate
conscious sections to apprehend by the title of single aridity
lost without market juice. So low beams in the picture
touching oaf fond of mere algae try living straight
or touch-tone or glare. Enough rage paid in mobile monuments
in a line of verse tolled in the glass below cedar trees:

repeat entry of the guillemots, their sobs then wire
at sea with no port to head for. How will common cement
set the promised line in a moving poem, they said,
quoting Rimbaud's angry poplars dancing up tight
and revealing how to fall for it, how to introject it
a drowned nuclear nut floating skin down
a corded tenderloin of sound anchored in the sentence.

Questions remain about absolute knowledge and all the rest
her grandeur let by the derivative image, spilled latte and limits
even say unravelled spectacles watery and frankly dilute
and not in the least welcome. Passionate she sees in time
seizes paper and ink, lady detail and heaps of clothes informed
by closer exultation and larking about in the clichés of political
economy and other binary fancies, what we call a tidy coop:

rest is for the saved, scolytid apoplexy and a stand of trees
is what could never have been pondered then, welcome as
rays magnified to the top of the scale, trailing heat and light across
bark and its exudations. Pens come from such a sick root it's asking
for tears and vomit. Introducing cauliflower to simplify bowls of food
did it. Nothing like sounds paint, climbs up a dark tree hand in mine
leisure escalating keys to the key without writing the door into it first.

## *II. Glossolalia*

Now enter the ductile beating of an autotext directed down
another logic tree to ur-names and obsequies for deadpan
strictures tightening down there in the bite section lip gloss etc.
Tell us what you would have had it mean, you father.
Proud element going up and over. Dance sequel
treads a shambles perhaps rendered in a jingly day
more trodden by the law of daily entropy than mine:

welcome to the rest of me incorporated part only
certain to scribe what was held in place as common truck.
A rippled quiver extended through the garden for press day
combining dismal right case by case as they say loudly
saying I wasn't born yes. Lazy gleams are aware from then
a skillet reduction for the people of the overpass, nothing less
than phantom caves always beside us in ground scent interiors.

Exclude Columbine as you must. Place a cryptic key at the end
of every day reject common mandates by sea or land seeing
linnets given by a wife to her lover as allegory related arousal.
Not even familiar face it and vomit and part. When you say that
it offers one law in a column does it, if you want to get a head
on your shoulders? A beam on the 'it' and how it is seen
on pale flanks. A posy or a floating place to live:

mourn the sea, abstain from lunacies in silent comedies
Duke Ellington cried over, their young bloody nature
on the make. Caves in us darker than a bottled past
to lessen a word. No is not a concept or a beam
of violent comments seen as glossy comments are seen
like decomposing glass. Parlour flags a passage down
a floating half-hour upstairs, in single file silent comedy.

Eat the book. The young Duke's natural blade created
the tune, the man you meant. A few rarities, a stone, a plant,
a daisy's unexamined leaf and jonquils and lavender
due some motion some force earlier. Go
roll a circle, see a nest, a determinant slice of she
as she raises her game, jumps back into a verse a cold
letter by a sunken jugular concept deaf in one ear:

take in the sun properly through glass like a sister of
Hegel. Sills agitate in evening treelight. Vesical
colour blobs in a theory of evening days after
manly proof edges the deceits of mastery to dumbness.
Anyone can see a fault invert a view of law,
stand outside the fence and your feet will ensure
the skeleton of right, vermilion silk waving above all.

Lakes shine to wink the blue air's stellar margins
like single apprehensions. An adroit comb-over solar
scene and a danceless sign of iron text eery as tree vapour.
Day's tract for all future travellers leave on shield two
to kill in a can. A smile, an agora, a lot of loot. Ivory seals
and sacks of eggs, gawp shoot or queue one more time
for universal petrol heaven. A spectacle leaves the sand-dunes:

regurgitated land, food of France, reason again
daily ring sombre daily pounds aching flanks of an ill
abandoned dancer, a sack of words, a lover (capital Tree)
single arising catches a crack to the ratio. That's all it takes
to form key ripples in any name, a key, a cry,
linseed stood in the leap-a-day dance, a lacustrine obligato
done to a natural fate. Pork eaten with flowers.

Foreclose and undermine. Sign seen writhing in the marsh
advanced against sound, same noise plays to a glance
and turns the viewer to stone. Do some vandalism
on flowers, eagles, campsites and stations. Fail us,
trick us, parcel real sensation up into a stink of nostalgia
cash machines arrayed in furs throwing up over the parapet
finished, unfinished no end subjected until nobody sees it:

it's expelled as a lion unless it makes comments. It's a killer.
Trade unction in the full glare of transcendence, nothing else
left as our carefully present dealer stands centre stage
initialling prizes bleakly like a deserted lover
haunted by blind fairground giraffes galloping round and round.
Or yet to come, a familiar curtain masking single lives.
See through this signed eloquence. Blow your gnosis.

Throw up concepts in the reception room. A beam, a veil,
a scene with no footsteps. Silence on a floating moor.
Swap places in the lunar comedy, Jewish, remaining, falling
crisply. The lemon you meant was a yellow flower
signifying love and *Zusammenleben* and squeals from market fools,
the circus's decision was a pure, determined cut, it
came down like a somersault and hid the other side:

joined in and out like a concept becoming a reason
or a raisin in its own glass bell, tolled for whom by Sister
Hegel who says a beauteous evening is real as food
in two columns, one theoretical and one actual evening
for other people. Male villages with master bedrooms,
seen from another perspective, stepping away from the vehicle,
the tank, the fence, oh fatal sister, fatal offence can kill.

Invading silk. One law for the military. Afraid of a scene
of writing, advanced mush of under-the-counter masonic props
and seamy stolen glances at the available local Medusas.
Fancy flower, cut flower, flowers of the forest, all
repressed past scented nostalgia for spiders and umbrellas
all finished. Subject to ending. Subject to invisibility.
Drop the flowers, pieces of gladioli like glass on the earth:

defeated, disbanded, displaced. Draw the curtains. Veil.
Whatever brings you down. Mean secret things, families,
sudden yellow flags by a pond, waving the law revealed
as if in words, as if with a sword. They baffle the limits
against the house. All we do at night is listen to the frogs.
It is private, privatised, deprived, disheartened. The principle
is to think it would be nicer. A single blow. Everything gone.

## *III. Glossoplegia*

Glowing on your tongue like shards of relation suck
and nip against or across the hundred-watt things you say,
at home address time. Law scrimmage tears like a pearl
of mischance and abuse. A sharp blue where bluebells clump
blue and broad and quiet enough to lay to rest
the veils of force and power to hurt, placed in a glove etc.,
glued or standing there as part of a composition of relics:

uh huh. On parade's a pure sewer of onomatopoeia
or a structure of. Unconscious analysis we call it.
The pins and prickles of economy wait to maim
as if food and glass were authentic terms in a peer report
or sea shore. Passed the age of religion lapping at celestial
reasons for laughing, soldiers fastened by words against
a haven, a dictionary of glossy names has inflamed the tongue.

Wrapped in rope just stay put where the whispers of company
in the campanula tout their regrets quite sealed in visible logic
like the man who called language a constant lute. Natural right
is mainly a slow fuck in philosophy, and it curses all surnames, props
to nothing. Tell a creature to party. See over the mania, don't empty out
the pretty coral, see the paper flower they always translate wrong.
About suffering someone was wrong, the tightrope-walker glows:

love of the wire. Skill. Prescient leaping in window country, comma, as
he fumbles it, dives into ragwort's showy waste of shame, all the people
love it, like the old town square, a pastis. Put another way, a double
death, an absolute, unmediated, over a vineyard. Ran out of time as the bell
tolled for Colonsay, the straight street dissolving in front of plaster gulls
and red wheat, say it again, that peroration had wings, it swung with
the daily motion of shelling ideas to place touch and pour on the gloss.

Island glimpses point to new scenes, to lights more pearly than a silent tomb. Preening like ducks, daily seas cancel out the shapes of need. Lunar bonds ask and command and disband the sand's due season in strict conceptual dashes. What choice is there in this serried line of V's, except to tell? A wave of the tongue like a curtain of blue peters out into portals of blather, as if to suppose a fraction of crackling interference under pylons, just picked up in the gloom:

no glamour in the toad house, he said, you betcha life those reptiles have NO taste. In this country the police offer up their posies as they slip or collapse over the unpronounceable key. Speak video. Want to shoot desire into dust till only the tools remain, frozen and glaring? Deploy discourse lures. Say what they own, their own potency, their own sense of their own death, stuck up there on a ladder like a stylized gladiolus, shouting out pink wonder at being human.

It's law in a glove. Up against the complicated scaffolding of universals
between dicy and dingy, a glutton for egg trade as the grandiose substrate
of social glue, they've built up pillars and columns and capitals into
a fleeting framework of sensitive power. It rises from the sea
with a bag on its head like a chimera and they hit it again and again
and the sound deepens, passes along the egg in the contract, they shout
for ligatures, push it with hate, kick away the afterbirth and gloat:

glazed and shuttered like a house I watch, at the edge, not moving
unarticulated, disjunct, and motionless. Out of sight. Faces return
in verse to say values may soon be relevant, get consumed, borrow
a village and dance the bury the dead functions, the death of distance, lone
magic contra loaded vine. Must be counter man leaping the time of my mind.
Once pork is firm sell a family or spit in its mouth, stay composed
all through supper as if it wasn't coming back. Wait for a glut.

Glad charges. Rapes, hunger and fear while Etihad and IndyMac can
juggle controlled family histories, angels spitting chain reactions
and sexual difference pieced together like Fur and Masalit in a
double bind serious hyperbole tracker. Very far indeed
and faster than Hegel's maiden aesthetic, you know glass
is never enough and vanity underlies each spicy motion.
The roses of Mallarmé require letters rather than glyphs:

the global silence of print on demand among the starry dews
a message washed down easy at a long cry, a beheading on the wind
proper buys put by for voter nutrition and a more spiritual view
free of lawns and barbers and united states of lewd expression
made for a wake-up call, wake up and lie down and enter
fake shackles in your version of work which is SO serene
it will lure you into a tinted art, or into total glaucoma.

Fields glisten and vanish, dead for par across the combe, calling a
betrayal of any free men allergic to ringing, how it tells of layers
cut into skin, crusts, bosses. A first reading of the stones
dressed to kill from day to day convinced of unjust sounds
in flight to sleep's veiled monotony of budget sentiments. Wreck these
devices, thirds that walk beside Fonagy effects, bent into oblique
poor endless cancers, isolated tents in each segment, each present glob:

each gliding self set to prance denuded of elsewhere, found in the air,
simply because of corporate capital deeds, otherwise untouched
unserved unprinted and illogical anonymity. You know. Loosened
by interlinguals, the bind cleaves the palate, undoes of oaten stop
in a spray of glands and tongue and mouth and glottis adoration, pivots
as one hand deals shiny with memos and shy as gnomic words on show
it's truly international, like a cut on the cards in bank plunge gloom.

No rates now. No glib writers. Firm in font prison words
at last bells audibly off parody as trebles in metal are meant to be
prussian blue as your sea, are warned to take an ethics rap. Or to
clone columns, clone shared cells, pick your own, own your own seed,
just as petal prinks a cut sky with cash and its own limpid sheen.
Down on the dish, cracks elude the circus of reason. Towers face
shut skin, the rind of right after Antigone's death. Nothing is here
for tea. What I meant was the glaze on the tongue, the glucose economy:

so have a glass angel and rip it open. One mercy monster, a link
tenet hurt by it, and lost for words in gluey deferral in the first
place, like a walk-in larder. So say nothing on demand, partly more
in the idea of ear as a contagion in the phones of consciousness.
Measure ready for a rest, punished in form and in case of work.
It comes back to laws making bodies do things. Committed to paper
like fishing in glass, go on and never stop to utter gleams.

## *P.S.*

*Home in the cochlea silences pose in a veil of movement*
*as sea-edged stanzas reveal their thought-twists and fragments of sponges*
*and at times a vertiginous leafiness raised to material status:*
*crystal flowers combine and a helical thing with a closed tube*
*moves one move off through my fingers, a species of mathematics*
*heard now as bells like the gulls where curving and clockwise forms are*
*composed for the length of a tide-change. So shells are essentially fluted:*

*disclosing folds of the whorl of a greeny-blue word in your ear*
*as it's glass. If you stop you can hear it right through the bone to the night air*
*to a tip from the hand's own turn over to all the beginning's*
*lack of these stones. So that cutting across I think of a tissue*
*of acts composed of our shells full of coded visual or spiral*
*echoes the colour of molluscs, slighted tone slides of sounded*
*words in a haze-lit time, in a shellfish seam of blue noises.*

# TIME DUST

*Equipage, 2015*

*for Siân Bowen*

*Trying a series of keys in the even chords of yellow ochre light*
*Hold down each note and try to prolong the willed delay of night*
*Then holding the idea of darkness above the furthest nape of your neck*
*Reach in through dust to measure the texture of what you thought you could make*

## *Title Disputed*

Felt release to blaze what to flex
Wet cannot doubt by law or
Count out licit voices little noises
Paper rush linen rusted stiffly not
Walk up under what roughness
By hand to mouth day plate
Taken a part of what felt here to
Be over this in light dried or more
Thin skin to fall on top by stone by
Feel of it most coarse time public
Walk by woven view of light
Weighing seamed a stitch in the time

Bend in water and tend the nest
Left here to spin so in the stream
To rush down side narrating its way
By touch of cross weave where
Tender is as tender does floating
Blind cargo soaked for days and
Nights some vein of violet some
Stained light moment of fear catch
A stale whiff like old bread gray
Fingered tough with the smooth
Recollected in tranquil pigment
Now lost in the white of thin space

Split ash as dawn splits now
Goes on smudged into baking cloth
Over dough of doing it from in
Side feel it again on your hand
Warm and worn slid in place under
The sun for each step shift ashamed
At such easy starts and jumps
Great sea out of mind dredged up
The petrified forest breaking fast
First stretching taut against breath
Strict warp bleaching where sand
Is still wet from lost water

Edge unfold to a shared band
To spend like time in rubbed
Bond limits left level of erosion
Worn lightly pencilled over
The forest floor spine laid down
Flat where she excavates bone
Needless or pointless so one knot
Joins points of red in the end
Young grass in the felt mix up
Fold rough buds solid in logic
Yet less than a while on its own good
Wall blanched and smeared up

## *How Things Are*

There is no such thing
to see is not simple like
a portrait some must die
helpful to return to it
taken for a kind of case
climax of knives to be real
to be used, to be added
I do not say right by
fledgling right and solid feeding
but also in relation to a certain
clearing of the whole site
that she did duty by the age
blind and frightening past
the burnt house and yet
the trees still green by
harvest flying in my eye
past time to shed the fresh
study of fact finding pleasure
like an umbilical cord
enough to burst in
the night, cosy jaws
that turn out badly

in all human fields the minute
the cloak of space of guilt
paradigm nexus done in soft
pencil when I am only torn away
a split stroke of dismay quite over
took their solitary way out

Both parties not content
are being ignored here
beaten up by an Irish rebel
kept out of it their just
remains of paper label
shows no overt signs just
skip along or in a pit
neatly folded at least close
where I would have put her
treat five days earlier in print
illness and reflect disgrace
on to a fictional gale of rust
free hand in happie union
to be discerned dusty struck
off lettered by hand in coppice
shade tree by the faded writing

# *Wood*

A paper gazebo once
a thin sheet of sorts
quite silent in the wood
taut to touch drawn
materials of approach
rested if there is such
anywhere to be touched
drawn by a finger
drawn up into being
made of paper, rough
by moon-light or desklight
gnawing at the eyes
their slips of emptiness:
looming stillness bulk
of trees and soundless air
with stupid apprehension
paper waits pencil waits
wash waits for a look
fallen away leaving
cracks and bark to
roughen these worn
walls for reflection

and its burning process
called forth, called
forthwith, called to restore
and draw the light again
back idiot boy back if it
emerges through citadels
of earlier works by air
or sudden dint or slip
touch it, touch it back
brush it off, old paper
akin to folded air in the
place it occupies
forever kept as aware

Now stupid gaze away
turn to one's own thwart
bones to prick the sheet

## *No Tongue*

Make a mark almost of
simplicity to need night
at the listen terminal
rough up the surface
a bit more or gouge
it now all be just something
up cannot be and yet
to establish foundations
for say identity cards
what stoic consciousness
within the present phases
the distance of modern
misplaced as well as it
means this illusion a mark
of aspect in the ratio
punishment to another line
with real folds over again

So again see what it brought
to time this time of common
honesty, the portrait of the dead
figments and fictions in the absence

to whom what had been in her leaves
even my own ear for a change
nothing but managing and presenting
for shallow things and short-term
goals an occlusion after all that
like shiny books along the shelf
glass washed by rain to look through
at waxwings and bare trees heaved
in terminal patterns on moulded paper

Gasp. Grasp at the air dots
in between the linen, think needles
think burning edges, think through it
and confirm the pencil trace
down in the corner believed wrongly to be
identical in each instance as it utters
its scribbled purpose in letters
of smoke and its stupid commentary
stares back robustly at you

## *Not Quite Time*

Now that it's dark crumpled grey
to black air creased paper found
paper foundry gone to light up

rapt what rapid rub it wrap it up
on paper like this, wrapped in a tension
place of dust lie down and gone

no time emit light in a blue shift
it comes from there did we know
this where we are in the dark still

to rest on alight on it by soft friction
made it up side after side by trial
and effort look at the glass not me

askance cut can you see now & dried
by night fingering what it is smells
burnt border moved slight sigh of air

## *Still Visible*

Absorb it like ink, the dark, the distance
the cosmos on minimal array to undo
a medium of access, to coax brightness in
to locate the feel of it where it was folded,
where the pinprick of a folding star is
drawn through from the back to the overlay
of choice material stuff,
a torn subject

Poor thing, go to her now and then,
lost with discarded paper in the unfolded forest
in a drawing of the sea on pigment
laser cut to prick it. She cracks in its wake
crumpling into the form of it, its new form
thinly covered open end to end
moving light to scrape the silvered shape of such a dotted
refolded choice
by the glass doors, scarped
to an inclined and honeyed text:
look in this act of fragility
and see how it is as much like reparation as it is like lost
trains of thought

All white to the horizon, wheeling flocks of birds
over ice, over frozen fen
flicker as
I gaze as if on paper, finding the grain
of it, listening to the track and
occasional objects drawing their space
around them in the cold.

Time. Space. Habit. A line across, un-
touched on the very absence of a container.
Diffuse everything you know in a web of holes, the thinness
of things all over the skein of the snow. Ochre, sharp green, grey,
slight bands always here
burnishing through too much glass
diminishing as I pass, doing and undoing
like ash settling. A puzzle
exact detail up in one corner, a flat field
of floor boards unspoken under the wind turbine shadows

All fleeting,
a periphery glimpsed flitting, made from these floating paper worlds

## *Last Year's Light*

As if it were a membrane
I was showing by all this light
how the senses of birds
leave aside permanent anger
how to explore the destiny of a subject
how the thread of a tree unfixed
and hemp paper in support of it

This light in space where damage
pushes it out with burned fingers
emerging out of the paper
like news of a war in Africa
emerging on the paper or into the paper

Transient light mirrored by burning
any hint of human existence
gently cracking, groaning
in a replica from zero, a gap
in the compacted books
created in response to the ground
closer to home and more minute

Thousands of divided landscapes washed and separated
into modern discursive forms like ribs and rags and lids
How much longer can you look at them?

## *Simply That*

The steep streets and the window
this unmeant mystification
I've been down a peg
where the ice slowly melted

in rain-muffled air the bells cut through
flying into the right word
the matter in their own shadow
Earth's immeasurable surprise

fearlessly crossed the parquet
the bearable film of life
the one bare tree in leaf (elm
tree bole) unalarmed among sheep

But you weren't theirs to
be the carrier of torn grass
O keep it still your hand
the sky would move in almost

blow down the flame and ash
so much I would like yours ever
the beech trees pierced and sparkling
seem a small thing on the air

## *'This Umber Sea About Us'*

lost in stressed paper
scale and the sacrifices of form
as time to verbal power
and rhythm of geology

a sum of something years
in which nothing left a mark
not of a human mind
slow as a cluster all present

in an act of making marking
time as a sheet of paper
hold it to the light
and see the normal condition

echoes and flaws in my pace
ordered curiously in my story
recorded on interior maps
sometimes confused with houses

why have the means when
this always outpaces us
and the place is a sudden air
a sheet of poetic universe

ready to leave something
between sound and objects
shapes cut or burnt or pricked
stacked up and never safe

this umber sky about us
has done its wet work and
light makes a rough surface
void under shaking fingertips

# *Avian*

Flat over to the view's edge, wet to touch.

Human inventions are pitted here
    to a decisive art newly seamless
or whatever my book cannot
            claim to envisage as causal fen

                        Don't be so startled
                                    emergent and arbitrary bird!
            Such sounds in the air
                        sway the reeds as they stand like pure threat:
look and call into question the lived mess always present

Two or three idle alterations to a hawthorn
    offer a nature of gaps milled by winding to a gate
and explain the point in that case of matter and power. Everything flew
            up to be otherwise, a different nature handed down to me by my father
                        as free extrinsic wild plums
                        split already yet for all the world
                        like one, quick, to sharpen us

## *A Film*

Give against the grass. Stirred clouds. Flat waters and trees
were still as a mood and a fair field of thought. Reflections. Like
it won't do what it says on the tin, and that cruel issue stains the light
with a film of realism. Anything may go wrong enduring transit
to where it has never been, bobbing through water,
slipping with desire by bond and word of mouth propelled
forward into the dark. Words can be said to stick with it in a snippet
of verse or clumsy tongue signifying in two minds and two tongues,
a conflict offered up with oil and water, fire and water, cascading
across the stones, drowning the grass and leaves until it thundered.
Like it was by the skin of their stone, sun and leaping light rolled
round in earth, rocked in time to say any floating thought. What
ever next we might yet have to sip may loom like language
weft for me, warp beneath the soil, upward fluttering.

## *Deep*

Try for blue light under glass find rosehips awry behind
          you in a ditch a distant ochre light
          soaking blaze of grasping for late truth
finches rise in a cloud fighting off the dead idea up there

For now deep gives a little membrane in the autumn
          light outpouring to the wind over
          unfinished views you dread to see
dropped pools under black peat fantasy signs away

Such poor expression lift or tinker with it as still
          sheep gravely safe by the fence will
          stand or huddle to make a nation
hush and let fall words of such a feathery substance

Call again blushing knee-deep in letters and beads sent
          too far into the night until a knife
          smoothly comes put it down cut us
all off from it all take it away once more from the tip

Call again letting go just as you like the source for sale
          photographed as you sat there
          no less than under the skin moving
in blank lapses invisible to foraging as a novel remnant

Gaze at plaster dust as austere insects take hold
          and cloud shapes shift the patterns
          of vapid thought close chopping down
to nothing but small waves to represent in a similar vein

Time and again time's loved trash falling leaves us where we stand
    at one from surprise turning again
    or turned back to front beside the wall
nothing but unfolding as was meant by words better said

## *Easy to Say*

Now in no way be without fire, or a subject place
if not a machine. Dream to be able in all its parts
and find them so before her even in a surrealist poem,
a lovely bit. Would not exist in this emergence on a
couchant of its own, but even that won't suffice today
if it is complex, ionic, broached. No organ play. Only
painters from the moment one speaks one's tongue
to exist, just a little well conceived, a marsh, a few flowers
and the sign that reads "Reality serves no purpose"
in front of a wall. To say to the person, accept it in
some direction that hurts, don't hold back for the end
of politics, organise most of the time, adopt a new style?
All the changes that issue lay out modes to escape from
an idea. It's easy to say, visibly twofold, but in common time.

# *Red*

The window burned by fire burns the landscape, the far
fields, solid trees, still river. Air full of insects. Swifts.
A bronze plate, hanging. What happens to walls and their
awful message? Is the edifice built? Or must you stamp and push
in the life's work, the pointed boot for brevity's sake
and the jumble at the frontier? They create their own world,
a dark background that they call the acts that shape their own
dark world with no inside to call their own but me.
The same goes. Like the war in the air, like an order, like
nothing in the distance, blind watchfulness, a face with
eyes that turn like a clock within herself each time
you doubt it, out of reach in complete recall of the stars
it goes. It knows its freedom like a damsel-fly, all the while
knowing what would happen, red, at last, and not by accident.

## *Fire*

A more popular guarantee of character
caprice and passion clearly manifested

not even one formed by climate and
better be cut off by financial incentives

we believe in the state in a mix of fact
a touching faith concluded the cast

we like pleasures to boost values and inner freedom
in a home-grown culture dredged up as realism

who are the little unrelated vehicles
mourning and bubbling with grass surprises

despite innocuous prints and pictures
noticed to one side of open war

a great deal burns brightly and lasts
procession further back in time than ever now

# *Corncrakes*

To flee danger dissolve senses to assume
the realm of forces and ourselves breaking
from the top window discrete small stones
as one thing to span space in order
to assume items noises even weapons
at work in us then vessels to yield up
no further edge (but why does this occur?)
unlike not a thing or a number in which
we party to escape among the stubble

signs lie in a wood ontological as echoes
a patch of form never done again entices
the gap in it in sense as scents change
to remake trees and weather or walk
over muddy earth crushing leaves or else
double flux to open the trap in order
to exist or arrive at itself under the sky
in a book clouds pressed into the binding
words streaming past like cirrus on the wind

inhabiting outside like paving stones in space
we ask the ink of the clock find the cone
gone at the top time left alone to come
round held back by the same weak passage
drift not thereby in present time and never two
always as its own misery and migrating to
this phantasm that we call the ear—yes
grating like a spring or a corncrake on a hot day
wavy air grasped and certified as a true likeness

## *Drawn Shapes*

*for Jenny Diski*

what only if this bleak refusal
cracked drawn wishes but between
the feet lost in a map of specific
future wind from which it fled
must know how to look not to perish
to sleep on real fear and think
of this here before me spouting
a staged fray, a not to be there
by which it has been limited and so

fluid and cold anatomy lessen
the factors in such a way to add
any particular angels or pyrex kind
of divide milky white before dawn
involved in such heat not just so
to look back at trumps and scales
in large rooms and the sum of stones
but later rhythm in the same flat help
and not to vary in its rule

so far so outset of the first sublime
by a new pace no more a thing
untied of spirits matter next above
in the first brink in all its thing of years
or it may be one plan of human process
of the way a human empties as adept
in time to link with the shift of item
of waves and ties itself as plot across
and ever out of matter wave or go

## *Trace*

Folded very thin about their scissors
durable, dipped into tiny metal blue
lines with abstract foam collected by
the string boxes

imagine closing your skin into the work
of running eyes in time: you are lost
or uncommon, silent and alone, no history
of touching hands

she worked with discarded wildlife
to be held or touched in their own body
refolded through the feather, cut and dried
like a glove turned out

these cases aimed at the verge by the glass
give it the aspect as well, it forms her cue,
does not depend on the action of light
from a black surface

where they end up like a phantom paper
in danger as they slept on between out and
crackle on the balance on a mould with
string of the bark

she has watched in brilliant rags and sets
at a time when it was intended
very carefully untied fibrous and soiled
small shed particles

drawn by touch and recovered bodies
relics about one book traced at last
as descriptions back in the mind more
or less uncongealed

what is not there was drawn or traced on ice
with shifts or shows through the damages
close to the border of mapping these stoppages.
Find what they need

## *Crumpled*

Pull and mean to spare or do for
tender notes to know a face and add
what sealed apart I do not know

later drizzle from a vantage point
as surely what is needed can come in
a letter unsigned to do my failure

or in other words go on as still as string
coated or marked or woven through
thick clematis and a clothes line

stretched to touch found objects
in solution hung up dried and found
again in air or mind twittering all

order in patient fibre lines cut
or joined in a film of something thin
within it all a stroke of dusted light

stress crushed to ink layer after
air on paper fixed to the wall
as material for a time being

## *Light Paper Material*

Passing may be in the sense or ground under foot in
a terrifying search. He should listen. If he is made up
he must be. Perfectly if we get peace we do not get it
simply in nothing at all to happen to think it has been.
An open door from memory is the mere art of the wild
and where is a bomb? Under ice try to read salt or cold
words. It's an occupation and roses or clustered birds
and would do better before we know how to be met by
light burning things. It is even and can only do damage
in our need to be at the front devoid of stone printed
structure, leaking crass assumptions. It hurts. Retinal ink
burns as the sparrows cluster and squabble by the time
of one fragment of one seed. If there is a mystery
it will be delivered now through the air by twists of this paper.

# STILL LIFE

*Oystercatcher*, 2015

*To whom it may concern*

## *No Way*

No way to compare the very place
this sense felt before with pure breast
or self by adhesion among cranesbills

but at risk to restate or stage the world
of difference between the most difficult thing
and a life to imagine taking place between

one black bird and an other whole way
It has to be destroyed now and then the object
the roots tricky as you know what to be

a song flying by sharp in the ear true
as heat folded in waves and stuck as threads
silent as butter in the stunning noon light

empty gardens burn and beat the air
too long fledged in flesh and bone to fly
to a terrace of words and anxious jackdaws

## *Warning Ignored*

A cup. A thin white house at night raised
like a first patch of grey breath. Enclose the end room
the sand's saffron lines undone or urged back. Imagine
no more than the rest as chalk and silence. Sun bubble
on mind up high, be a girl. Go down to know about
the house with me, at the sea, by the bed that ran well enough.

Assuming the end, the wood, among other features. A country
lost among blue and yellow tiles, balances upset as from the
world over, too up and down, a best man erased. Can we
burn oil and dust by the Greek sacrifice? This all began it
never left to stream out far yet, to come in only in machines,
eyes open, eyes that hop round the same in a new rhythm.

To be new, not a part, not destroy or make a description
I went on. The rain began flying quiet across me. Fear a man
in any rite if he is at once lost in a mask of uselessness.
Common and other look after a hand open or tight about
a wind from nowhere right through into the earth.

## *The Mode That Will Not Be Written*

Once upon a time out in a wood
I told you it might be better
not to be able to find the world we live in.
If only I could grasp old magic to work
in much the same way one means
to be taken for a model in truth and value,
draw the line and leave, immutable

Our attempts between formal realities
as a notion to decide attention on it
hurry away embarrassed for the light.
We might say the name of all the scope
deserves the way it is in the mode
that will not be written, and I determine
the writer of controlling desire

But suggests all these forms are mere
questions of expectation and so on
led into the others, not touched.
It is the custom in speech and perhaps length
of time to perform pattern or require
panting and growling, alive, sociable
and impatient of the series

There are others more like a ghost in
monotony and clumsiness, looked at
closely on the still white world.
Moments in motion from which issue
limpid silks so the letters can be blotted
unquestioningly in trying to become
changes in disguise as ideology

The death of violent respect capable of
activity in such a hectic book creates the
shifts against aversion schematically.
Gave them weather reverberation because
the surge of verbal time smothered guilt
with one sentence from codes in milk,
cf the original right sun rising

We feel he bites, passive and ready, through a
framed sexual glance and manner as often as an
emotion to dole out stupid, difficult colour.
Rights of others, varied attention, waves of clarity
exercise the will, the look is straight, no conceptual
voids press a world collected in attention and due
the figure I think has been qualifying him

Everything else is designed uncertainty or at least
a peculiar violence between the land and thinking
so that the effort will do and be a self.
It has no idea. This scene seems to begin between
things here, develops into difficult self-possession,
emerges to contain the writer it asserts
but only in means to which written work is the recognition.

## *Seedy Box*

Time I began to try the texture
in a kind of idea into other things
closer to an image of life, matter
searching, bewildering, ebbing
when we look back to the wash
in the glass, clear blue risks of fidelity.

His father cracked back harder
agonies of a world like writing
the phrase to permit the key of
a cycle across the edge, not notes
first but fitting that it falls after the end
in a French poem, mind in the wake

Of fiction in the next end, the way
the mind is night, that particular night
after it whispered to the end loop
and questions to endless debris, ours,
burst rarities content to divide nightjars,
apparatus, semantics and depth slipping

Across the surface of the world. Say times
are empty, an entire life lost to expression
of the end. It pulls me and stops before
a nervous twisted leap and claims the blind
friends in secret failures on the page
crying in an empty past, rustling desires.

Water burning could be a put down. A work
of art. Cross focus and flee touch, a surface
by what they shape to overcome the words she

portrays. Life in a mirror would mean waking
to read as if from love. A web buries its surface,
spells itself, and buried thought replies…

A climb to the floor to begin maps of the body,
burnt clothing at the door, at the window
shade to the left of details that elude the presence
of little boxes. Air circles in an act in my flat
book of that stay. The actual form in a seedy box
is a case of statements in this poem of consolations.

## *Night View*

It was too much like a knock, hiding my eyes in
a radical night view where the patch for the box
suddenly lurched into my heart, awake
with pointless ground after all the days
it will never know will never speak will never touch
the lid or infinity, or taste light from stuck space
or wood or field or train or pain that

points through the body more than the desire
finally as in this pure matter terrors ride. I met
the matter out far to show me the effect of
the same as me, just round the corner. She
uttered the word home to help such reasons
to a clearer sense of grief sinking into the sea
left by some strange pink material at rest without a trace.

## *One*

Silent singularity by a real structure is not
interested "anecdotally" over and over, it is
a sustained sea that does not last forever, even
to work in a new key, since the heart and magic
could resist collection and shimmering. Necks touch
striving for silence or fading or extinguished
to follow what happens to know.

Every horizon begins again, no choice
about it or its own false device. Black coldness
with dents is pitiless as the world's deepest screen,
as recursion, as the rooftop's relentless echoes.
Combined in motion I might endure but not finish.
Flat light, thick with my clothes. We uncover what
we have illuminated, a clear surface in time.

Photograph of beeches recorded in a single blank
world. The spread was a later archive of loss left
by a scene under glass, icy and undesirable. A linnet
pipes, leaves home, remote for two or three years,
aloft and circling in a slippage of personal pronouns,
falling away to prevent suffering, the things he did,
harm in a home almost engulfed in fenland wind.

## *Image Damage*

Not thinking about wild truths tied as to a tree
left him deep in love and neglect and stinging nettles.
Remains lingered in his speech, slightly warmer than today,
interference more or less easily leading to mist,
muted to pollen and cultivation cleared by the law,
trying to speak of love in a vast and unknown time,
to be read, to stop as our own, to not ever be, again.

## *Brown Paper*

I don't know whatever it was too hot and dusty
behind brown paper on the way down to speak of
wearing black out of the city to be brutal in for ever.

O watery and impressive thought, excuse all I say
boxed in until the black plans for nothing to be sent
on to serious terms of guilt with requests and demands

arrive with daily blares and jabs on the air we breathe!
Let me be a bit less, a loop artist, an earlier work of me now
out of the way and edited, telling more to his own first loss.

A figure tends to break down. There is no ground.
Tongue to fruit to printed lips is clumsy and might be
endangered in a pair just waiting to explain what I want

Who can't see. There has been something up to a point,
better than others, a style out of a job, the brunt of my feeling.

# *Footsteps*

Evening was an offshoot in my memory to which
the poets said nothing, moving off to crank up a voice
motionless and broken up. I lift the stream of my kind
just in front of the clouds of drink, to grant as she was she
would be not so, edging, imagined, and found. Back now
without life at this space of my memory, I thought in
two ways and in speech. I was a mistake, paid from
the point of view of trace and waste. Plunge. I did
what I did yet the footsteps that I knew begged me
to write another world, all arranged, led on in a circle.
A face, mortal, mad, like myself. An assumed blow,
time fell in a silence on the side cut short and late to
the door. I remember pain straight there, how it started
in a strange wonder and personal dream, as they do
dawn, and made it this revelation, driving the dead subject
as he testified that night like a rush. I tried for years
to speak this that now seems even more so, yet just
swamped the brief space I liked so poorly. What shall we do?
Upset after a stay in earth, so brief a time to see the letters
I held, watching them breaking out of part of me.

## *Empty Space*

The organs of evening space
name limits to a person's mind

composed on fields
his own sort waves and he

warm and disgusting
looks for hours like information.

The first melted liquid had been stones
to save rather than money

or a kitchen fading in the rain
or a spiritual look in business.

Unconnected with each other we meet
quiet and thoughtful and rock a little

regretfully round a building:
I'm not sure what it does but

it leads to quiet panic,
the view up the whole street.

The mountains
can be pulled apart

hidden beneath lace
summer and winter alike

just because we had stones
where we could look up.

## *Cold Again*

Books in the shelves creaked like windows with breath
dark within bounds to expect a point in this round idea
against her whole time, cold again. Powerless stare
to press the unfair evening lamplike images all the same
beyond the rude voices. Tears happened like a stumbling
after a ghostly woman walking down her own face
round silence, deeply. The woods were wet and scattered
to touch the edge as the end of fingers in a secret heart
was spread once by his wrist. Autumn earthed it up,
the sky lifted off gently against the tree, shut a tide
with his eyes now only where I heard it once between her lips
as he saw the wrecked wall of careful irony. Talking to men
was fog and dissolution, the lake or a photograph in lines
a bit open, that floating tired light seemed to fade the people
gone, an infinity gone, touches of life curving off some other way.

## *Rebuke*

It glows with apt light in fabled waters, from a story
he would tell the milk of words when he had fallen away
before the days. About time it resembled the place
and the attempt to suppress it, part of the long evening
of underground matter in which the present is narrated
on the streets of London and then withheld. A way to go in
recast as a relish factor in any case, cancelled and more sedate.
Origins, patterns, clues called in and attributed to bites of rigid
links still in circulation along with the ebb and flow of what we need
to be told as a more distant piece of a present. Grasp this
and find it as real time profit. It can be uncertain as whatever it was
received by the eye to disturb a power in my brain events
will be voyaging to trap the work of words shaped as if it still remains.

# SPARE RIMES

*Cambridge, 2017*

*'Even a distracted person can form habits.'*
*— Walter Benjamin*

## *The Field*

There is a field that will persist in everything:
    what means crucial means
if there never was a thought deflected not to be
    a path so far gone?

High in the blue a buzzard or two gone,
    mind or brain looks down
or sees impediments as trees inside the skull's
    plain journey on foot.

Finches dart over lavender, the play of light
    becomes dogmatic
even blotchy like bubbling water or white
    clouds gathering crisply

Over a valley. There was a path breathy with
    things unspeakable
or words for them, prickly bushes in the way
    from a time to time

Pushing you to go south. Or somewhere
    radical without
ice and its antique functions, chipped syllables
    in a needle case

You could say, to disconcert the writer as
    the path vanishes.
Ants and lichen on a tree trunk occupy a mind
    at work or at rest

Thinking like a glimpse. Over the next hill
          a hot-air balloon
or something floats, a far concept finally
          attains its rhythm

As the clouds grow. Wild plums also grow
          visible clusters
at any rate, small fruit happily found
          in another part.

## *Of Art*

Not there, the power of written signs
stripped of their leaves or colour, lavender
scented letters like far clouds discarded
and pleased to be so expressed
as a butterfly on a leg or a ledge for a moment
begging today's question.

Spare moments gazed at walls of exaggeration
yoked with too many dimensions
in a sort of Cook's Tour of time. Roof tiles,
Sky dish, waves over houses,
insistent buzz above my ears, lost among
the close crowds of entity.

Silence broken by water. Still deep folds
holding material thought-runs
under the sun, green against blue surrounding you,
breeze swaying the tips of branches
as bees dance round each other in the air spinning
thought out of light and gold into straw.

## *Paradise Lost*

Shade at the point avid for light
        avid for water, sun on dry stones
avid for lizard flick, avid for fuller presence.

Can it be done? There is no silence
        in the night, no rest in the dark
or in the mist outside the window.

Dreams someone tried to explain, avid for
        reason, avid for meaning
laid across an ancient pattern of fields

Harvested, avid for growing, avid for market
        returns, as we are harvested
while who knows what's growing beneath a surface.

Hum of a plane, chink of a bucket, goldfinch
        chatter, small noises in the sun
shape my thought like small grey moths in the grass.

Avid for rest, clouds gather after noon again
        light bleaches the roof
dry as the roof of my mouth, a few cicadas

Somewhere, or nine stone steps. Paradise was lost
        as though written down and left
behind somewhere, lost and avid to stay lost.

## *Saturday*

Empty air is a distraction
cut out of another void
scissored away from cypress avenues
and dusty white roads too far
below to see anything in it
that feels like thinking or flying.

As we could be, now,
through this shiny air swooping
on details like a camera or a firefly
touching down for a moment
on a roof, contact lenses or sunglasses
pointed at a ridge-tile.

Looking down on a valley, go
higher carried on thermals until
each farmhouse rhymes with
fieldmouse, perspective awry, your wings
shrunk to angel size,
curved and sleek cut-outs to keep.

You call it a drone and you might
be right, these days what soars is not
always the imagination or the heart,
and seen from above we will
always be a distraction, a target
for some process that needs to cut us out.

## *Loud Bees*

By the fringe we gaze through thyme and leaves
at nothing. I can't see what thoughts look like this
          not yet, on the side of this hill after the clouds
have disappeared, leaving nothing but lightness and bees.

I could imagine the problems solved with a little warm olive oil
before the next ones arrived, disguised as butterflies
          with short attention spans, allegories of anxiety
coming and going across my field of vision and yours.

They sleep though. Everything else is alert, people even run
and I'm always surprised by you, often pleasantly.
          Self-sufficient, more or less. Some of the memories
are orphans, left with no thread to link them across the system.

You know this is like justice, and you say so. Let's hold it
there in the attic. At the edge of the woods a door opened
          towards the south. It's difficult to believe today
that there could ever be enough time to believe it all, ever.

## *Where's the Fun?*

Can't you keep your thoughts to yourself?
I interrupt my wife, like finding a heron in the bath.
Will I ever learn? Linen is no excuse.

She was once a General. She's a tactical genius.
She wanted to be a spy but had neither the languages
nor the required duplicity. She likes to mean what she thinks.

The easiest way is not this way, downhill. Watch out for
strange noises, which could be large and wild.
The Pup might save you. In a funny way. Really, he might.

Still, war is a serious matter. But at the moment,
there's not much we can do. Go back to your homes
and buy expensive mirrors. Fill your heart with better thoughts.

## *Protected Wood*

A badger snuffles in the night
Of porcupines and stars:
A small torch throws a beam of light
On teeth half-bared before they bite—
Each body bears infinities of scars.

## *Not an Object*

A shimmer under sheltering leaves, reptiles and insects
at work under the sun, swallows and swifts away somewhere
unidentified above the ruins of days and nights,
with mountain frontiers bringing their own stories, too.

Put your trust in maxims like Life is Hard, listen to bees,
walk through clouds—nothing is too much trouble.
I think you've got the key now, so sing it right through,
while the sun stays behind this tree. The hours are for working in.

Stones on roof-tiles make strange bedfellows but only the insects
are moving this morning. They consume the small spaces.
It's hard to know what anyone's like behind the sparkle
but we all want to find out, pushing our noses into their pollen,

gathering it in the back of our minds day after day to make
a new image basking on the stones like a lizard
in a film about the violence of love. The shadows
are shorter. There are walls and wire at the frontiers beyond the valley.

## *Hung Out*

I didn't go to the airport three times, it was
a very brave thing and close to the bone; I began
to be adapted and synthesized, with huge rattling windows
            to convey my approach to my movement through space,
through part of the poetry world half a year later.
The pleasure was mutual and became a frequent food,
sharing this taste for puns in relation to politics and
a way of writing I can only imagine. She was estranged
in her small fabric-dalliances as her heart opened up,
benign and hilarious without talking. She rarely went out alone
when I was longing back and forth between capitalism
and the kind of delirium that places a model car
            on a woman naked under a table like silver grass.

Had I made a mistake
trying to be virtually anywhere
            while the others were just waking up?
            I recall passing in a void, all these rules
an attempt to compose dream maps, copied
on a freezing February afternoon, stuck
to my mind, trying to find a xeroxed mask
for money in one endless, hallucinatory sentence
about writing leaving plaster masks of their faces, just in time.

## *A Quieter Light*

Drill on through the day, casual and violent as a stony lane
in the heat. Twenty white butterflies on one bush. Coffee?

Can you make out the voices of the past? Something lost, something
bad, not good any more. They have been detained indefinitely.

Each arch its banal self, failing to be a fiction as yesterday fails
to continue its own trajectory into the present. Titles have faded.

No wonder. She thought of the word 'palimpsest'. Paintings in caves,
tracks through the woods. It was uncanny to hear woodwind

among the trees that day. A wild music, like the drill, or the big
black bees bumping and humming in the salvia beds.

Such things mattered, saved from burning in time and space
piled high with invisible bodies, where the swifts bubble and bank.

# *Small Change*

Away from it all, bewildered owls
above the pine wood's warm air
wake up at night in my sleep.

Frequent small incursions of a way of
living come to be hidden from the homeless,
the old and the drowned.

Between the lines, under the surface of a morning,
some will not arrive anywhere tomorrow
to lie down beside cruel waters.

Some see through these lines of sight to a daily life
destroyed by bombing or the grinning grasp
of some financial centre's operations.

Over the valley once, before I was born,
I lost my hold on air and fell out of time
on to these yielding bodies of hell and high water.

Butterflies mutate around us, bees fall
on the manicured grass, the air thickens
and cries at night like owls in chimneys.

## *Just Ignore Them*

Even the outline was hazy now. You know what I mean? Dust
of words in the valley, bones of words in the earth, pain dry
like lizards behind my eyes, spiky and watchful. Such distance
at work in the twisting air and then a single violin playing. All my endings
at once, dissolving like dream boxes in the night.

# BOUND TO BE

*Equipage*, 2017

## *Plenty of Nothing*

*in memoriam Jenny Diski 1947-2016*

Pale duty stamps about in plenty of nothing
        like the night when you knew everything to time
when each step was beaten off when the rack might add
        more glory and I would watch the stars
not kin nor proof to rule the sphere to know
        by clothes and tea how to cut them out of lino

Now see who has the little boat of love and wave
        adrift more salt at its best splash scornful enough
away on your right to curve well in some hope then
        plunge like blame, a hat tossed up and gone
and lost wires humming if ever there was one at hand
        always apt to walk with me out of my mind's eye

Old china caught to hold as springless nature seeps up
        and wells and brims and falls back again
in a forest of beasts where silent stories reach an end
        or in dark lists above the clause that starts to die
left to review by me my kindest cut scabbed as a free
        local disguise made naked to suffer for doing just that

You could give it up for hope's always a bit of web to ignore
        bound into the relief wire bad as you wish for
this lack of a figure in the grip of method on the screen
        to burst out of acid to be like last at the spindle instant
as a gripping vertigo flash vacuum leaves spores in place
        of humanism for us when this frolic unveils payment

End a hard time to get enough pink forms to reconcile
two worlds of the mind to say the least and work
safe hands on what we know to move abroad like autumn
leaves the trees revealed at last as a mouthpiece for language
a copy to taste such stress detail at times of less art chat tangled
to a dead tune in sharp clothes in a space of her own

Make one pall as another hand leaves another letter fail to
earth what it says out walking on skin debris from two
true stories in matters as if we lavish its fine tip on lungs of art
to put a stop to this tread or peg out between ruts
in thin sheen as that eye that glass jar screwed cold and dark in pots
too out all the same with a stump eyed from the window

After midnight it was a baffle or a very good copy in some style
stapled deep with a mist full of blood for free detritus
flooding slides in capital sequence to watch them drive stout posts
bleak to look at into the dark ground the black lightless fen
all about the aims of the whole bound in like a literary theory
snarled in rough cuts to earn a living to repudiate

The hoover fades beneath a lethal march off this page
to another partiality from the air against his masks
to form him now in terror forays or shape him in dumps
in flame run half afraid on a floor of damp glass a lip
at fault speaking idle threads down to the bona fide dress
shirt in hand over fist spooning into his face

So would you care to remain here and be consumed
round the neck as the only way downward like a load
of light verse enduring through barrage and fancy filaments
twittering in the ceanothus of invention parcels the
air bent into aesthetic shapes of this mercy or that or broken right
apart eaten away starved crushed old mad blind and stamped on

Late level force embraces anybody it's true and I must agree
        with you out of my hands to where the cities are power
splashed out in a witless sense, a complex merit or class say
        or ever becoming a kind of work out loud burning
it from one end to the other just because of skin declaring decay
        that might be a view from nowhere but a day in the country

What was made by us is hanging about covered in ribbons and birdshit
        and aprons all set on this time of night for any other way through
tangles of a seedy mind to hold nothing touched or even true
        to the same life just a door step away from a sheepish mouth
munching a sliver of something carmine and ludicrously
        pastoral as fishpaste or cracks full of dust or an entire bowl

Don't nod or scramble so ruefully for dupes or lying for the poor
        furtive moon-blush army come back to try the view a lone
odour of almonds: am here am you we're a monstrous pair of crows
        doubting summer's purchase a blush in a garden of gleams
sowing seeds by the ankle path to sow wind in the tender cedar
        a charm above the door dilapidated its charm raddled

And see off a dumb tally over a long night's counting till the sun
        gilds the new and sole account crowned legendary and lost
a film a few saw sheepishly on a blank promise to be better after it
        slipped inside to do as we go into the barrier; a face opens
the book of wishes and glides illegible as badgers in a complex pattern
        buries a bad label a gesture or tab scrawl I'd like to escape from

Oh secure fluid relief at your age one exists or leaves and will
        dissolve by final flux over you unaided inflicted and not once more
be ever one we hear so much and weep at windows in lost sentences
        ignored in the rest. The words on one level condemn us to death
of the use of them as we must simply know the part in the whole
        devoted to a singular being without being which there's nothing left.

## *Sunk in the Night*

The bare limit aim from its inner shape or the form of what is said
has put asunder cold dirt like worms on the thread of light
craving loss in a mist right in the centre as deep as a veil in sleep
the herald of crumbling as far as this new-arrayed way to knot the heart.

Called between two objects left out through its undoing, this is still
far from other sweet satisfaction and destroys a thing
that according to itself is both within the world and yet at rest
or rather time the curtain is scraps of paper stripped off a painting of
[content.

This is the drive up to the ending, a good cry bitter to be seen
at the ashes and meant to arrive at the disappearing debt as nothing
while the moon that shines blind from the start can delight in death
in a stupid lack of chatter, a bit under this that she was shouting about.

Come into play, write under the look taken back into warped oak veneer
or just splay a pledge like something far too disallowed for one evening;
cock your modest ear, avert your eyes as you do, a failed mouth to cry out
of the earth until there is no such thing, no wrong, no better aim to find.

In peril of nothing else but a person dissolving to an expression of the rest
from itself, this negative nature, this infested portal with its peevish crowds
is the world as flung waves of hatred, wandering ash in such a false larynx
that it smothers the reason of its purest form to fill up at a well of dismay.

## *An Ear To Cry On*

In a time of money, to look out for a part of life
I lost before I was along by my parents and
out of sight from our shingle, a mess might be real
cries moving back, thinking to avoid a torn city.

I wanted to breathe the sounds we were crying
by putting my hands together wrong,
but the rain was a cinder-grey window in
the bare room. I saw the silences.

Something damaged the edge of a cliff as I came
to belong to this view, homely sounds with
misunderstandings. Within a week I always felt
intimidated by music that gave comfort about my name.

I was hoping to catch my wall taking shape
out of it in a dull drift of settled money and time,
upset with a glass and my work, but there was a flute
sonata for the silences of breath all burgled and mangled.

It was form with my presence, my want in islands,
but I said no. It went aside for me in spirits raised
and bright, exit visas sanded to the touch coming away
from the wall. Years went by to dread my feeling otherwise.

# *Northern Line*

Never prickly air in the world was a late cry
shining to silence different ways you like
much before it was only matters, you know

Well, this was how what had got a little line
when pausing was her manner on fire, he saw her
cosmic and misread, imposed on more waste dread

Too often hearing of a puff of good reason opening
a balance after he had no heed in a blur or two
hitched to the unforeseen rain through to the ashes.

Never lie even at very abstract letters, type a quick
look and go south admiring his nib with a rustle out of
the loop with a view, say, down the Euston Road

Lines from a garden had the air of a leaf edge
rested round a pink wash pegged for ages in sight
as if I was a live grassy recipe like a new skin

I didn't say anything, brooding chords in mid air
quivering into a state of mind that declined all day
while the dark unsaid was too small and slipped to the floor.

In so much care for all the time to expect each round
word let's set up a pity of the shell, gone far to be found
after dark in the blink of a birdless turning life vision.

# *Old Details*

*for John James*

The old details rise and set out while years are made
much less certain by the first real price of structured doubt

All hanging to be shown on the hand of a banker
through a narrow street of his own, backing some fact or other

By the true company at the start, living from soon after,
he met this type at a height to overlook the picture I have chosen:

The open surface hastily arranged from bright sources,
the eye sees denial excluded, a series of trees, a sense of relief

He wanted a record of things as a means to use fullness
closer to the old blind sense, he needed a house there in June

To give new lines in the way to pool a short flat illusion
light exploited no mirror with the glass in broken planes

Roofs open into the surrounding system of movement,
the implicit meaning in a sequence of lines has been developed

No moment can overlook the reader, and then a disorder of bright
red came into his poems and created a bond with myself

It all came to rest in *Simulacre*. Shadows as paving-stone text
and a letter about revolutionary potential as unspeakable art

Work demands the rules of the game and death's scratchy lines
situate the shape of the words 'preoccupation' and 'once' again

Leaving the surface to walk over the air like this is so rarely done
that here it calls to mind invisible gestures made within its matter

Signs of the ordinary earth, the pale sky calm, integral, and blue.

## *Will Do*

Feel it will differ, even song
bodies large so they flow like
an immense elsewhere

No empty shoulder alert
seems mobile or stone
to ignore each by timing

My ears on the gravestone
glass mind hanging on water
would we stay the same?

Not dreamlike and did not
break sparsely. They resist
a dramatic container dock

Another colour prompts
living points to mouth
then it returns to being

Some notes float in the
illegal inner world now
come to say it could

Not have happened. My
last case of cast lightness
has far more to fall for

Night wish mostly blacks
& greys where I enter my eyes
side by side until now

Open space while shame
brings me close to daylight
and its forms of speech

## *True Rendition*

If I were to forget the rest in a breakdown of law
I'd choose obscurity despite my skin showing up
when it occurs. I'd lie on a table or a drawer
waiting to be slid away and give others the chance
to stumble belatedly or to stay for a long time
with no need at their core after all the drives
            towards this trope of true rendition

Later to pass darkly or enter the head by
distance from the line of the feeding mind—
as a meditation rose it is right to add infinity
for a thousand pounds of portable property
a sort of land reduced to the eye in a fine
melancholy lot of mangled limbs and dying with
            foods like sugar to lament and snipe at

Nothing sacred about doing this only in
connection in that form so slight in itself
less than one, it can be no question of
what one knows—in that it has to be given up
as a thing certain of itself as regards contentment
but clumsy with scorn and full of the simple world
            fallen free from the contrary side

For all to see a disposable system I had thought of
at the sharpest time to find schism-failure, doughy
names and baby shelters all immaterial after all—
it faces the past starting up again inside people, imitable
by none too close to the same ground white and hot
tips too many spills I mean to let it be white or not
            as it seeps in to my other ears

A phone cries —Innocents, shall we look
more drawn or flat to protect me here or shall we just
mean much faster? Can we? Any time over all this
gone to utter rest for a turn about turn over
and dial it out over a dull red mix. Please no
respecter of portions, grafted or bummed a quid here
            to sustain repeat blooms

Now see an old yellow cloud hovering around
the throat of art to stop around the handle
and listen to rude sounds like porn milk and jasmine,
a frame never boiled up to a kitchen idea. Nothing
really happened, after all. No pin, no gin. Poetry regained
confidence in the brassy and infinite like finches
            round a feeder squabbling

# *A Bit Part*

Deceptive struggles take the leaves
          to wipe a story on a body whiter than
the forest air about her even in her cage
          his failure like cold tea and cotton wool

to flinch from the bed in darkness
          come up still without part now for the night
liquid as well as clutching light can take it
          for the price at the back he might have said

feel unlit dry stones about them by the wire
          so it seemed to be part of a clock so by the sea
got up back in a wet spring for the regret
          by the wood between the snow shifting

so falls a more sibilant one on the phone, falls
          from the house to strip a tap behind my eyes
who had no feeling of hanging down again
          simply on a beginning of the end at this fury

split himself and others within himself
          straight to touch hopes and actual purposes
fed by labour: if you met him he might have been
          the self to come like Faust in these sleeves

mad about sheep and wind on the land only he
          can say more with mud and gravel for the idea
of simple words of himself hard on a fountain
          drains his memory for the rest, the part he is

## *Free Amble*

Dry light to boost the grave legal taste of the writing, why
be fucked, embodied in an idea like hand, meaning its mark system

Claim free claim protected, why one should keep the idea to pot
before one rotten break too fast and get just as far on real charm

Cut away life in cruel age order fluently, a common thing
held far back it comes in branch maxims, a most articulate nutshell

Marry and get them slow hawthorn and pots of cold grass
covered with out of work grit, no plug on her plastered teeth

To lose the last nail, soon belting out to the waste pale and felt
wild and soapy a second blot far from light, his empty eyes grin

Wet to a pit rigged down at his horn master, the dead bloom
about the child turns down to catch a house through the wood

You should know a ram on the line and on his father's arm grating
says she needs a little farce with tongs, her plot delivered from years

Eleven now, non other boote to catch, fog in a mirror or piano bubbles
a wet knot and shit rather than face it flies in the face cut and past him

And what else wipes spirit so dull that malady would strike and roar and fire
and vanish in dark air, a sharp nest killed and dressed to so forsake my
[home?

# *By the Banks of Grim Margin*

As I walked out on a glimmer of linnet chat
another branch of the unjust mingled with silence
at the front again don't trust a writer in shades
of blue the last moments of a level blue glacier
by transit with them distant from himself with them
between himself as on that very first day. We used
to have a house he said that skimmed the surface of men
to condemn the last set piece in blue pencil. If words
that cut like steam were all spirit all in play why
arm the flesh, why lick the skirt in your hand in a
corner cut to pieces? Only so as to lie still again
as an old log dead and found fit to work some dream
suspended over script like payment for time saved
by the banks of grim margin. It must be the last day.

## *Crossing*

*for Lara Pawson*

On a street on a wall with him and without him
or are we part of that word wandering? His feet
knowing had been through one place to another
for no one knew in that going only just the street
to look away fallen to the city, our need close by.

Keys of language, the liberties I heard would help
her because a world will never remit the one door
that level open rest over so far and so many weeks
of raw majority no bare earth or grub for food or
water by word or gesture not what she has left.

Destined to become is a negative worn down by
blood as we say as we were due to come home
we could no longer no longer remain on the earth
when we left them for dead in limpid water and
all it is said to offer and disintegrate and nail us.

It was not kind, a poisonous leak of hope as a
direct hit on need and fault and what can't help
who or what in knots of wire like faces and faces
like wire full of distance complete and near grief
to explode over again no chance to bind the cut.

To trim up for refuge brimmed grief so to hand
and always to fall back to harm of the living, as
we were born and are deep in us in the world as
a flight from what it is to what it is and find no
respite set in motion but fear of dying out of it.

## *Limbo*

*'Limbo always made more sense.'*
*—Ann Quin*

Window blurred the rest
in an alien town.
Let's be kept out.
The room through a keyhole
and afterwards detached ticking.
One blow
a single line.
I am, I want
nothing so contradictory,
the happy trio
under the trees
all flat awful counterparts.
That funny feeling
would be like the sea
between the railings
you drift with
bits of glass.
I closed his eye
by the edge of the water,
fluttered.

Look up. Under-water.
She peers through glass.
Nothing to contend with
no sense of belonging
a catalogue of places
men who resemble
it can be another,
that grey, grey thing

something gone wrong,
it's so late.
Another person another role?
What film did you see?
He saw the open journal.
Mist buries itself.
A father complex
a feeling, a need
observed us quite honestly.
Undressing quickly
on the spur of the moment
I could see it wasn't,
for days now the rain
a whip in each hand
objects in that room
lay there, their legs
while she looked in the mirror
in this city, obsession.
Lucidity in fantasies
the breeze blows through,
I am completely lost
out of the day's rhythms.

Contradictions in roles
we assume shape
her by the elbow,
something I had known
on the desk before me.
A vast stretch of sea
rests on the window sill
in her dancing under this sky
at the edges of the world
I was being followed
half buried by sand

between tall buildings.
We were misinterpreted.
The sea a faint white line. A longing
between mirrors naked
he knows she needs
parts of him
that soon perhaps
we will cross,
subject to change.
Into the huge waves
she threw her body.

Come filled with dreams
a waiting between life and death
a time bomb, a 'love nip'
for your artificial heart,
attempted touching.
Please write soon
to affirm any order
I have ever seen.
The other looked
at the other two,
the moods the three of us had
constantly changed
between the three of us
until we arrived.
That place that did not exist
that place in your
piece of my own fantasy
closed my eyes in philosophical vision
as it really is.
I opened my mouth
but no words, only
my in-between operations

the words of others
chained the three of us,
motherfucker.

The sea
sea
where lights are stars
slowly undressed,
she fell back she crouched
she looked at the door,
she alone feeling
patterns reshaped,
dark eddies from the green
how it will mean
the space between
that's the third
between the mirror and herself
couldn't be seen.
Did you want some love?
Impressions stain fears.
In the doorway
the house was in darkness.
By the time I reached him
the machine
which he banged and kicked
naked, emerged from the sea
then the dreams came
dived into a huge wave,
spaced out, stopped waiting
the film slowed down
away into what is left.

# *The Works*

## I. ONSET

The strange turning arose at his birth
as if my brain was glad to run from it
for the poets after him greedily lapping up
will not create the ocean
though ships sailed round about
they would have been strict rivals
as any boat could tumble
after it had relapsed for want of the shore
the sands there for the first
the second that they burnt and crushed
the third thought eaten up
in all the distress in my head
when thought will have a mile of it
but this common heath lost
and a flying voice dispersed
it is the winds and the tide fled from us
walking in her streets
scarlet and unquenchable

## II. HEARING

wood or iron spits
delicates, wash it down
the river into gold
and that was the first time
you have read these
false leaves on my foot
let me see they were
still sucked by owl-light
the blind sea-side
a cage she desired
found a means as
the waves dashed as fast
and break the eyes in the tide
bread and moisture to cart
and cast away the trees
must belong and be heard

## III. THE RED

Five to one in the balance
taking the shine off ears of corn
gold never shed or perish
out of their wits. Small things
never coloured as long as they stay—
O, it was a brave age then!

## IV. HARDNESS OF HEART

skins fast over a heap of money
face light as his legs above ground
five teeth, the art of old dog,
the raw cold air will smile upon no man
only the number when

## V. OUTCOME

set against the ample water
he must swim for his cloth in torch light
not at first as most flame about
the whole body in his time but later
in the foggy smoke a book repurified
in alchemy of foam or froth
debt will violently break the entrails
and I am not against it
strife promised no demur no syllables
in the smoke wearing a cloak
as if by no lost memory
a knitting up to clear my tongue
things flow discourses of my secrets
the whole matter sprung with the breath
hear what he could say right or wrong
utterly not suppressed or mentioned in a volume
a twitch of red in our nostrils
quenched his fume of double weary dust
no money should part his reason to make a sound
against briars and bushes against his will

## VI. MAKING SALT

The common good remedies may be sure payment
but from every one of these I dissent

## *Saving Time*

*for John Berger*

It was called a hand as proof, spotless and caught
like watching a false cuff, kind of. It is a pepper mill
or a path like a vision along to the glass door. Her will
and the men, hesitating, end up like a house fire.

A tight fit bolts and lands in such a way. The shape of hers
seems to me to lament mere shade. How to paint more
of a given social role or type had nothing to do nor to believe
before the turn in time. Nothing can contain itself.

I knew about the grey stone and vegetables carried in his sack.
Writing, like the habit of meagre eating, taught me about exile.
To be a help he took my arm, white hair, ashes above his destiny,
he made his own way in his studio, a lesson for the future.

And when I told him, he imagined the dark coming back
until the sky flashes and the hill remains after death
even as you chart a future edifice of words. Do not explain
rags of mist and speed: the eyes are closed to hope.

## *Could Be*

A kind of flash put between the world
so touch locked finger in the wine once
now to grasp in two into the twisted eyes

Folds in string secret hold up the window
but above all a smudged mouth that foresaw
shadows when they came with a touch

Up to his own love with a moth letter to me
a musty upset, a glance down at faded attics
day and night burning the chair up with his eyes

Twine blazed from her spoonful across with
a squiggle loudly left through the door in stony
nothing that it was a seed she had on her lip

Poor cotton insides like her own body in a
private picture that they were painting in her eyes
roofs black and deadened in a mask missing her way

The window facing the spot became impossible
as stairs to the blind, glasses aslant the pink flicker
knew there was life as each of us die in their power

Left behind in ours, uncertain, sealed in case this
grief lock could be a light in him soon, when these
years were living unaware of any ghost senses

Too full after some childhoods and the act of reading
to the sea, late from the place slipped on the face
by her body, her head, gone now, letting the dream come.

## *The Scar*

*'Green darkens and | imagination fails.'*
— Michael Haslam

Body turned like grit only to set
 its form as fact in a gutter in darkness
if we can call it that, what can't be the last
 particles of air, of representations
born to argue and stumble instantly
 wanting the edge-stained place woven
and slant, now met outside it all undressed
 in time unsaid behind trees and alone.

Crisp air caused far wounds like far
 woodwind sounds entering history
with bits of shrapnel missing a snap
 splintering surfaces into some apple of being
scraps to speak for everyone but nothing
 more, a sign to shift for himself, a united
front fantasy of an actual taste of hatred
 blind to each other's network of scars.

Anger out of time in a singed skin in a sense
 of loss within the frame firmly locked
after shocks held fast in my case back
 in order, cast back into deep air laced with
somebody else's view to afford a true cascade
 of thought falling through the trees as light
to call out in slashes of green, some quiet zero,
 a place on the level ground to lay one's face.

Not much was with me since the name
 trailing between earth and actual silence
fell from the mouth. Instead of becoming

solace the figure collapsed in a flicker of
quick taps on a window, on the day before now.
Rolling the other half on my tongue
I felt the wrong part, I was about to efface
my share of the freshest side by side.

I stopped the meaning around a world
I thought of, a light bell wringing it awry
all from the fingered past of limits. Not
to dwell or break it out in whimsy fanned
by hissing light, a piece of puffed money
or some darkening screen I'd seen before,
but met by quiet law, a trace to bear unheard
as birdsong that came back in particles of air.

## *The Progress*

When we are born to discover the gate by words
we come out without them every day and eat the earth.

Come with him, left in view for ever when my dream
was standing at the gate to let in half the other.

When would you bind a reader by my veil, wrapped to tell
the way I went, in his mouth, in his walk, so little he did?

Out of my mind take help, face the door and the sound
step to the ground of the place over and above meaning.

And begin thinking a mind in a skin, or talk in so many words
as to neglect time, then trouble him in the room, cut his hand.

The bonds happened right, fast as flint through their ears,
with a worse fear that labour lost after I left to go past them.

Find spiders in their faces, flowers in the fire, also a bird like water:
I need to be the voice of my mind to meet the gate in my dream.

# MARSH AIR

*Equipage*, 2019

*The air itself is one vast library, on whose pages are for ever written all that man has ever said or woman whispered. There, in their mutable but unerring characters, mixed with the earliest, as well as with the latest sighs of mortality, stand for ever recorded, vows unredeemed, promises unfulfilled, perpetuating in the united movements of each particle, the testimony of man's changeful will. But if the air we breathe is the never-failing historian of the sentiments we have uttered, earth, air, and ocean, are the eternal witnesses of the acts we have done.*

## 1

Its very silhouette was an echo of fancy paint
approached on time, I thought, to drive hands down
the throat in a second with nothing much to tell.

Off in a whistle soon she was forced to write his type
so what must scarcely exist was drawn and died free
of air and local looks back into the time of this.

Better ventures rock in flat belief and he loves the
feeling used by lines to remind him of remains to visit,
or to fling as a piece in the sack out on her only ground,

yet then talkative in the open window curving down
like a curtain on themselves and a book. I eat and read
wraiths or moors, thought tones madly for a moment settle

like steel out of my face watched to nod, go on folded up
with him. Rest was strange, a fret scent over later feet
down a flight for all to go and see why air terrifies a name:

as well drop the skin pinned now when this little stage
broke well or couldn't fancy down the feeling before dinner.
Just halt there in the wind, as so often death may come up

on one of these days caught by a note fired three times
then resumed in front of his own attention, a life to be held
on the other side of the wound after things rigidly said,

without saying which is such fun for all of that waving
in a burst of unsuitable light or panic reduced and removed
to babble of what they call a seagull glowing and passing.

## 2

Another fall stopped before a live sky returned to
pick the lock they made and entertain an observer

red and grey the evening so local and cruel she said
meaning not much use of the first person in the old days

restive strides fail in uneven squeals seeing the subject
now vague silly book open at the village page still uncut

slight corneal damage in shady seclusion across what
they planned to be a door there across the room

a quake in search of the right words for fire and colour
to gage right whispers never in this to give over and go

in the act you came from, now to plant again violets
and roses in this floral talk before spring might return.

*3*

silence that shades sweepings
interpret the cupboard for him
not the right sentence, forming
in the room its hours each day

turned to a child with feet gone
on much as before imagining
I was not on a scale of one to come
to know or devise one for me

not for myself standing by my hand
the remains I'd failed to say
I could have set a single glass
in the flat to be known as pieces

of voice to hear how it tuned
to open the future glass or trap
the wrong frame in my life
posing like a group of arms dealers

but too late in value too right we
were so taken to go just as a bad idea
closed my empty voice we all make
to match a look as I knew like a shell

skin gone to a last shame waiting
with a missing name to be called
best to use the device by the spark
sliced in his field set to drop late and

merged by lines inept and knitted
he knew were to be seen on the usual
question before the array turned on
your self to have such remote failings.

*4*

Measure more intense times also but not the less
to step to like much that I must and is a violence

sharp like a future way back hours I let be further
in and so known and giving answers in fact I listen

as time arises formed of use as clearly seen as though
it does help everywhere in pieces of words back to

hero school like that substitutive play inflated before
the link dissolves each seeker slated on the roof

and stuck with posters like a night of stars so little
meant and does not leave any in hand or bankrupt

stock just deft where faces left remembered angles
under eyes or looked at vaulting looked anywhere else

at warmer air in places turned upward disregarded
maltings belted by hawthorn or a book of record.

*5*

Some hum for the good drives wrong from the sun-spread
window bewildered as exiled rooks now stand their monstrous
fading eyes, oh, to see what pistons draw my feet to face nothing
like hard feeding for this place like light aged dream walls in hand
sprayed with larks long risen under the sky wound: slow steps
do not hand in a few beyond hope of colour where once was glass
in the night to watch for the close there in the hedge over me

On since from the same case my mind in the post, an hour of the rat
against the irrational clock incumbent. It wasn't to be traduced.
They ask radially, rooks dropping against the rock thrift
landscape in all honesty in a plain frame some few strokes upward
and all to play in neglect protest for once islanded now: dispersal
talk all ineffective, let go my hand as when in my boyhood it
failed as it always does again erased or overlaid like a shot shot back.

## *6*

Finding rain detox refracted and bottled up
may beam and burn the sentence carried out:
hope remnant numbers still now just explained
how outwards a great other air arose.

It arose as May ended, heir to nothing but
numbers, dead dolls, curios and melons;
squirrels vanish as the angel exits in rumours
of the solitary lure of days admired and left.

Feathery doings: mute whispers dance in the mire
true doors open on to, a nest of surplus
mourners gallivanting and chanting yBa names
over the pageantry in handfuls of rhythmic oohs.

If night means fire it doesn't pay to drop a word
in the lap of care. Negligible wrong accords that way
back on a slab well past the least idea, a process like
peak thinking we prefer debunked and lifeless.

I imagine mutable ears and a glass wall, the next
means to an end beneath the map of cool sincerity —
nothing but the next public offering from the heart
of a seed bed classically composed, soft cool and moist.

## 7

Born memory interlude overt topic change
As a boom dangled over the roses
Reading paper again for some tomorrow or other
Breath over trees and dahlias, lost and disclaimed
          Under swifts high above the house
          Under no clouds of badness or
                    Elements to blend with hope
          Like minted béarnaise with the lamb
Will remind them to know better
How a system can hear how a plug can mean in a sense
Coming straight into memory, punning
Your hopes on it, looking at all those ruses, a
          Nameless canvas, a red splodge
          To copy everything unseen
                    What it includes banded together
          As storage excitement
Healing itself at the end of the line
Only now beginning to unravel all the time
Lying ahead in a later language they once had access to.

## *8*

Over it all means facts that things might form
work on the flux of a photo album,
makes it turn out clear to hand and twirl
with the remainder to face instruments of itself.

Down misty or enslaved paths at the same hour
might turn out old mould underground so can
we all redeem the familiar sign, source of biological
visions to own and to decide what pivots sway away.

All along you care for your order to another to speak
nothing at all in spite of wounded people or depth
in a civil relation who laughs all pressures past his own
not having lost the split moment of all I long for.

But what jars ungrounded bending in first pursuit
is a term to launch commitment fast with a new body
on his part, an angle in the mass off the air or on it
in a personal form of action you call dreaming.

So take on each façade of speeding cloud, crows rage
at a level of abject spin off the air between, left to
a vote. Nothing like an injured crow | to set your sluggard
heart aglow. All lids are off enchantment reinstated.

Look carefully at what you've done. Come back to earth
and choose and use your binoculars, kept awake by mumbles
about what they do without the aid of shape (you told
me in the usual way that it is not a body), and just look out.

Fixed outside the aftermath like artificial snow a bird
lies preening the form of money or something, a visible
test of the fruit of each possible book in a chamber of
thought deaths rolling on as you might say almost for ever.

## 9

I sang use and touched the pain theme for a time
plush by the sea on a weary slab of solid plan

and supplied a machine to find the rich obdurate
and smooth with wanting. Big and easy they pressed

with ribs and ears pent never better than with an elbow
at the air of sick sleep within the open door at midnight

with grassy sheep needed quickly by the elastic spring
of fair prospect. I found my arm doubled up to poetic pace

to track a plain eye into the clouds that tone ancient music
and lull the mind of rock with a livelier harsh and humid peep

at pained silence, in that it affords envy for me still never
far better enjoined about us without a tree to shade now

and if we step on dark knives leaving a name in a few passes
each one is various, lost and shortened and shining in the sun.

## *10*

How come the bar to like as it was found
was down the mouth about the lack of sound
I asked, and heard this strange reply:
        Now more than ever in the grey damp air
        the former walls are rebuilt higher up
        out of scale
                        rough to the grasp of wild hope
    like cartoon minutes in the original second sky
no words to roost in their looped ruins this time
    or ravens
                        to plummet into one of them.
Leave off your impressed grin for dusty tea
        to end blame failing in a later flair for grief.

It must have seemed all left in light, best asked to match
        early habits of the country in milkwort or tormentil,
        between the stones no grosser selves cut off
to verge on abstraction's great era, considered as
        near as possible to the fire dash, still out of what
                        the world calls scale and flat with rage to live in after all.

## *11*

Such days as now forgotten developed else
where and remained missing went straight to
a blinking hectic blur of light as now on leaves
is quite the solo entry in a vertical shaft

About twenty reached there only to fall from
what seemed same and lasting to stop longing
stop resuming or attending to another cold fall
from such a stressed pause level it was almost a wall

Now two such when some such same reverse must
lend reversal ties to memory in dark view the head
say against this rare gaze might pass for about one
in a son et lumière fest of ontological fuzziness

This small condition of being outfaces the stillness
to strike what there was ever that in tracking down
its changing prey was impressed better than injustice
elsewhere still the changing heart of what looked like light.

## *12*

Intent on one to multiply a sudden voice from an old
dream into a murmur I know, the time is bits and scraps
to understand how always geography could be animals as such
and be more than you must be every day to always last

Made out of the blue, others buried in earth or turned
to ash at last its humanity must begin to listen at night
vigilant under the ropes to question words that like stopping
for breath or saying what pearl that lukewarm adjacency!

A further moment is an instant now above this brief stay
to uncord all the regulated tracts of time into something anyhow
alive in a mouth and its heady movements. What now happens
in spite of the very calm aspens finds each the lower witness

The movements they cause humanity piled with age dust
with more forgotten words in their satchel eyes and dormant ears
rest briefly by my more than only slightly known headway
trying to utter sackfuls of no stone untermed, no stone given to the mud.

## 13

You may still physically hope each morning but not for some outlandish
round of hoods pointed against better round things clad to withstand
enough by will to obscure every ill-made comment flung back or not.

Reality takes minutes to arrive around saying so breathe no morning
was swallowed in a need for instant prowl round evening to spot what
they began before form from weather crannies made herons awkwardly
stuck into the lane where they meet small pools strangulating secrets.

Where do we go from here now the law is in its own hands and dismantling
all attempts to coalesce? Rain obfuscating the distance shifts the syntax
that used to structure it too badly for convincing staging to occur in a sudden
major key and induce delight or even more limber movements signifying fear.

On the wall a face for travelling objects falls aslant a dream of equal rank
bound deep to febrile bedrock times. Such powerful fictive darkness now
clings to the horizon, humans washed ashore kicked back demeaned by terms
no amends offered as shiver trash and grief coat concrete and heather and the sky.

## *14*
## LUCKY CLAM VOLUNTEER

*(for Rich Porter)*

I try wings in the air experience clamped
delight to lay bare small noise
flutter killing all they could one day for
some toothsome mob as at times
they believe by little urchins to end places
derelict luxury with good ink beneath
the soot of walls I knew completely gone
past another accident as far as a
new sinister role late parted or less expiated
            than a tragic basis in both names

Best now to hold the shell feathers athwart it
and love it at last among vast litter believed
to be wedged here until an earthless life or airless
country only cast pavements rows old hospital
planks back all found again by such a captivity
not refused and ready to grant such a choice
bewildered and constructive eyes in such brief song.

# TO ACCOUNT FOR

*Face Press*, 2021

## *About the Dark*

Controversial as for an innocent and open
miscarriage of speed as sound as less or all
we could explain, why it had to work on the
volume loan story of his plan with his vast
cost, ardent readers or any trick on his own
charge source; and his account is different
to give it clear notes falling to help treat all
the echo context. All apart springs solid law
tasked to pain material speech, any books
to a rise in the language of appetite to life
between two deaths pronounced and over
written as nobody has ever done it before,
books of unimaginable size but no meat in.
This is the dark. Part of ordinary workings
because of night or the cage while it lasts.

## *Look at Them*

Glimpse twisted look back struck expression
burning apparition silent unreality unwinding
a late doubling apart from time in the letter as
weeks run on eating the future today, vacant
last dream abandoned all odder reason to
dread each flat trace to occasions knocking to
improbable standard silence. Waiting bravado
shadows glared with quartz bell expression of
hands as intruders prepare to speak, confused
calm sigh to go back to even happen better by
acorn movement ignored, forced into being,
those on the edge burning where they must stay
in part gutted by the roots of quiet let far in the
trees falling flutter space cut by white sky over
my eyes, rigid obsession to care to come up this
uneasy hour to talk one way when I had heard.

## *Consolidated Uproar*

The security exception text measure or crisis
in perfect times of domestic debt purchase,
requiem chair not yet grasped as we only now
dismantle this drain rebound epidemic behind
the counter backed through language-networks
insult, my whole account loss is to be swindled
by fertile grounds for dormant set allocation in
nesty hedges singing like nightingales in the
dust, well I ask you. A call is specified and
not in use. Strain is a secret looking about the
problems I got to know, a wryneck in ivy hardly
seen let alone heard above all this clatter reset
as separation from silent musing a few years later.

## *Inlaid Reflection*

What noise supposes reason nod towards
shoulders in the past few weeks to pause
again by the letter pool, escape very near
wanted actions in the street to divide and
want others saddled between a time of this
or that, liability being when past returns to
begin here in my life mostly among ash trees.
Frogs disappear for shame if not against
reverberations, by some tug from stone
terror jarred again at dawn, all in motion's
embrace and lines of code hurrying back
to hail the body effect, footprint in mud,
slap as it darts away from the register and
off the record. Now inhale all the fragments.

## *Just Thermal Slash*

Hot days review ramps without some forbidden fern
refutation close to hand, nothing to lament. Leaves
if you say so all away from the bank like snow, like a line
surging on words for my brief turn early one morning
just in a flash impression to keep broken in the dirt,
always yours empirically or very well may serve to break
the ice as goldfinches do. Lucid strain, a table in need
of chance gift scales, poetry for economists with a word
about time by the window to empty lattice arrival of
the fittest, curious to the question edge, now completely
consumed. Splutter away, too good to be ivy, too old
for voices spilling rage as dry leaves temper a ground,
boots in the dark at the same time plainly heavy with
a need to know. Owls may be sheer expanse of air by
the field, not much choice, even wonder against hope.

## *Faint Last Abandon*

Turned open on dead wind consequence to
walk down to the better house in a way not
less than I could follow by ear, by switch access
to deal with land broken uniquely. Wait to
speak time to power, breathe to stone, hold
it in mind, mark wire shock wrong at the end
or wave and drift as you would say at my wit's
end. Wit's end weddings. Hark, hark, the lark
in another world. Right up against stone, cold
presides, held back to yield whatever's left of
treacle or dust or abstract line that hangs about
bracingly unused with rocks and stones and
damp ideas of spirit music. Do what you can.

## *Intuition Rush*

Thunder ruffle tip down sleek leaf shadow,
just another blackbird singing bits of rusty
air, slip to jump up still warm at the bridge
I mention now in front, now forgotten,
only to recur as it surely will under the sway
of fonts in fragments lost, particles clasped
to echo watery prints of appropriation
that make me gasp in pale strips of breath
quickly known before traces of feeling
sink back at the outfall. Abandon hope all
moving things snaffled equably in a sort of
moral balance attack on network sites. Slight
ruins quake to rid the world of all it contains.

## *Allowance to Hand*

Another time abated, ages left for me,
left to my choice regret as long as talk
felt by display to occupy or deprive fret-
ful manners, paid language gloom always
more anxious and under-theorised in a
part detritus filter, part citric thought
pattern of long shed struggles writ large.
State of change, herbal profusion, bees
bumble and hum in petal tent labour,
act mirror colour shift rain dead, time
of departure noted, new mint label to
print. Foot first twinkle at material text
substrate ready to hand it to me as if
nothing happened against the future
darker gloss on flotsam coating swells.

## *Coppice Fret Verge*

Pose trickles slide thoughts framed askew
down the years nothing adds up as super-
imposed presence all there still and gone
for what it's worth. A desk, a window, a
garden, equally framed. Think stamen or
stumble and stammer to jerk it free, red as
verge poppies, frame cut back in strictures
sharp edge insists on. A kind of farming
since you will anyway invest in clouds if
not clods, voter registration, boundaries
of the self macular or spot-on for so many
thistles and dandelions. Tap it all, turn it
on and see what grows in flat texture field
ground down by worry, gaps alert to call
about bat whispers and other lyric devices.

## *Overt Ruffle Return*

Over at the last air pressure gasp, gaps in everything,
even three at least graven in space as they say to resolve
a discrepancy. Now they fall like apples thud-haunting
each sound dropping slow in grass scythed for the time
as steps promise to slam it all home in lexical antinomy.
Grist spilt over night's doleful train noises, what can it
mean? Tailor's chalk end-stopped, visible shell of thought
going pink pink, social distance among the leaving airs
so sweetly set and graced, guest vision lurking behind
the form to fill in with a handful of earth if you'd do the
rest in peace in your own time please. Do say what you
hear about the ride when you land behind the screen:
plastic system at a loose end, beware slippery surface
curving back through brambles or nettles, odd memories
liable to flood and cause distortion or feed it back.

## SHELL VESTIGE DISPUTED

*Broken Sleep Books*, 2023

## *Orpheus Says*

Kind rules as blind as words see far indeed
and state all traits agreed this form does not yet
model change blown want as leaves assigned
delusion or some version of the real contracted
to require marginal eyes while secret arguments

sustain a way to feel about invisible force to pass
for the sake of bay or nightshade opening
a breach in wonder winding up to vanish or infuse
a deadly Spanish war's image with news of home-made
violent sequels shown on screens in minds each night

more largely bound to overlap cooler turns subtracted
by exchange of reverse tradition no less than a hybrid
verse flower more fully used there as its tension trusting
naked desire to read how margins hold the gate or wait
as vestige of some older wrong, the title lost in weed and rust.

# HOME JAMES

## *Something in the Air*

It might be my other image to cling in part that
I owe later to great acclaim with a blue ambition
snare to seize a passage in words of space mirage.

Rapt extremes bitten to speak so at the end of all
the years chances haunted by a nail inward to a list
of anxious benefit and any rarer payee approaching.

But listen, times to his last well straight to what posits
all my signs behind shutters again, invidious idea of
limit shining at each natural hand as signified on this.

Expect invasion in rococo sacrifice proportions, all
white glass and special drift, a treat observed at first
as a mask image of desiring fresh earshot companions.

Had I no answer? I said echo sheds the real word
called intimating matter in debt or believed it all
just off egotism, nobly right since we squared being.

Stake anyone in notice by one pounce in the deep to
clear it up. A loose handle will change your view to
show you how to name ground appeal tucked away alone.

He walked to listen to distance shift in rising attitude
until we bristled with dim elements by the spot of air
known as recital. In short my imagination snapped.

Chance absence led scarce space apart in the air to
travel by lure or menace fitted to her credit guilty of
a mute encounter before lunch for her larger order.

Her front pretext is glad to keep things in the tone
to assuage contrived panataloon fun, forced to meet
a particular affect she ignores by seeing fears get out.

Interest on my side hesitated by a snap of minutes
to draw the world, weigh the trees to the useful class,
talk from the house through a notion wound up to wax.

A flag of light turned actual rupture, a scrap of art noted
till I rest, watch stopped, need on the terrace exposed
conditions clutched in different silent work in language.

Say taste dropped the last birds in the grey wood
pausing in prowl or stalking the approach as if a picture
of a secret lantern before a sponge to keep clear now.

## *Nothing Doing*

Yet lucidity was lost in avenues by the lapse of
a margin to vibrate my last remark so my mind at
the end of an odd memory dropped field gestures
up my deeper sleeve. And there was nothing in it.

My own free straws moved in refuge with a shade
quite yet as a change by law to form old presence
and drop a minute watching a long revolution lost
in so chill a taste I wanted to recall the juncture of it.

I asked why a grip results in proof in space, deepest
matter over baffled scruples full of refuge state in
smoking shadow. I asked too much of the instinct
a formless touch in a wave of velvet gloom sacrifice.

There was something of a time step before we could go
by the smoke abyss dropped in paint, my right to private
wonder, my step a trifle apart, equal to that in another ear
for keeping room to turn away with no chance lost.

It was stupefying. A desert displaced on the spot
with a click and spread to a single wreath over rash flight
without leakage was sure to serve bad work or strike
back in her hand. Who needed this vast memory to speak?

Twisting night can be against sacrifice by putting up
a house of cards. It all exhaled a question. Tell me my tone
when a whole hand of personal state seems still a reason
for taking nothing to gain in a corner of your crisis.

Recollect my state for more news from dead delusion
with instant speculation and candid words to act under
in another place, a leap full of fools gone wrong, spectacle
held in a fictive exchange by the inner liberty of feeling.

## *Peculiar Pertinence*

Nothing lasted to say inevitable in a flash. Collapsed once
for the account, my levity ventured all they don't embroider
to do justice in the act of horrors like strong eyes in his state
of thought. Vagueness was really the whole air, deep trifle.

Question this thought in breath pressed hard about the spot
with deep care, an instant to rub my spell without a lie to still
nobody left. More to save than my system, your logic, my
darkness, on the free note of time and its form being cast.

Revulsion deprives the odd ground gaping with inward echo,
to effect matter now and lift a case to bed in patience. Down
for an instant in a glass and granite look while a fresh shadow
was fitted along the ruins, my figure watching their order again.

Pile hands now as if it was not too late for your stupid idea,
see water before you imagine matter as anything of value to
shake from the moment's scent of dust, a pinch of your time
to match a question of a place gouged out and left, not to have.

Look at the word and then sort it by light and weight, sharp as
logic, as flint, as sound itself in minute touch of the present
array gathered to smash the weight of years of my own, sense
left without sound, the last word done to prompt escape of tone.

## *Planted Presence*

Felt matters these living in the grave of his fears,
a help to an alien, a lateral flame of present air
by the general state in a year or two of climates.

End the rest by a step to avert scruple to call that
element a mind left in the light of analogy found
still in the habit of darkness and sleet on her nerves.

Damage touch accruing, obscurity of matter might
stretch amends as burst vision nursed in silence
to pass by the risk imputed to wound and defeat.

You might confess to pirates, know my finger, show
words in action choked out of a book. Dry it, shrivel it!
Any fool does know you dream of gaping interest.

Pull a shapeless object up a wall bound to the last
time of her strange name as a balm for a price of pity
worse than to drop away the minute it offers hope.

To make up lost fear and expose the knife in case
spoiled chance jerked to renounce an idea of cruel
justice, an aid to the first word for possible even.

Why should we dream of cards on his side, cleft for me?
I offer time as theory to use as a nutshell, to remain
to strike lucid matter in another flaw by actual attitude.

## *Implacable Grasp*

Fortress trash after a blow to live up to as if
instructed for old eyes by venture where things
work to his rose array illusion as to his face .

No bridge after this break or wince if I can do
a miracle count meaning time without desire
then to remember the door, a last light safe.

The street took all sense but he didn't pass the
end so much as gain consciousness of a question
reflected such as to step on another state he found.

Time on the spot would connect the object matter
in a letter so far as the question was back, studied
and cold, each closer day dreamed as apprehension.

No home could be this ground of death free of
voices in a chapter to mark a material fact like fresh
illusions at its feast of air in a word of poetry value.

Short glow fallen to its property of injustice nearer
the word 'stake' and a less silent message beyond a
single part of the face on this ground lived as a chain.

A desire for an order, new vision, a modern threshold
of disgust. To have to dream was the time to enter
the day he never counted the desire of time drinking them.

## *Nearly Stopped*

No scale in the eye of actual intent to get back a word
about ghosts of commerce as secret bounty indebted to
books had even a still winter law person to clear up. Less
in view for so few night-persons as not to have income,
a fancy house, a street-lamp into his dusky eyes for the depth
he was to have to hide in his dream for an increase in time
to settle given excess in hours, or to regard it as language
missing the day at once. Go so far so wet, be a time subject
in renewal, in other words be constituted by a sacrifice scale.
So new to reckon imaging of traceable connections never
let be at this last bargain in place, signs of length falling into
a wish to better the inner voices, his vision of the rooms of
his mind organising to waste time with an idea of his own.
The interest in his queer hand throbs in places dusty and
incalculable, meant to settle his special gasp. A day glimpse
waits behind the vast night, letters dropped into fire, a nearly
blue sense of art mistake, memory of latent space by the door.

## *Lapsed Step*

Artless space had to start a world to remain shut up in
after the impression by mere point as easiest breath
a cold square frame, no window, distant light.

Air as element laid bare past service, dropped straight
from a kind time, missing turns in a deeper care as
time sank in price tables despoiled without the aid of style.

Brush shadows into shapes like iron and oak, held moments
saved in so far as they suggest sparse render in lived wrong things
a tongue above all matters to test as it happened.

Hover with the cup to dose back all the dips that might be
figured as moments a seam over the view to resolution
so what was his mind stood new without the nerve.

Heard for instant tap of certain words to live in being less
alike, less painted, just art going to the verge of ferment
As the occasion watched for was at once quite affected.

This out of scale character had been sense let into distance
windows to face a painted figure, air from time settling on
motive refusal, the first thread of the age, nothing afflicted.

It was best within the frame of eyes turning exposed to dusk
pain on the wall, a lost face credible to hide, scant marks in
this dark view of desire. Time could only last under complete vision.

## *More Measure*

Force ease to assist at chill suggestion of a world
of dark escape, pull living air to smoke, sort by ring
tone as fancy nimbus at the eye, quiet fashion by
any case in one of the windows by night and fire
light square for a prowl for final human company.

The key to knowing action now would be chatter
made up to reckon without time striking alone in the
flame of this doubt candle, this minute, this trivial
insistence of light in a crisis, half emerged round the end
of March at windows by the level his eyes lashed at.

Morning exposure going out as if open, the inner
instant catching itself in the doorway of dream life
descent upon self-recognition, head stranger than felt
to be so beyond sense as his own upshot. The idea
divided a present shred, a poor vegetable diet after all.

Some felt form should know some person dropped
the key back to life for time on the occasion as might
any person elsewhere without action of his own. It
was kind of on the spot, difficult to mention later, tones
aware of marks up his sleeve found as secret to the brim.

## *Least Ground*

Nipped off it may be as gage of protection
a margin turned back for the issue of matter
(is it my own shape at the same time of doubt
all being scarce and losing it through the window?)

The grave was blank, time ceased to be solid for
less to exist as strange impressions of the gravity
in me: you can catch his voice by his sense of the future
through this time of given wonder in his tone.

Words trip them ridden by chance for more able
space at the door in this rain as it strikes down
pleasure in case this idea mixed less in that with
all you want to be inferred from a charge kept in.

Further stress delay and any door closed a little to
lurk after being through ground for all the world
to go on. He had to count each strike for provision,
able lungs, a fresh chill later reduced to proof of speech.

Whatever felt strong was pulled up to keep it dangling
in the least mind to think of, something like words for
motion, and leave by the grave of doubt over the world
waiting far below. Come to the door and plunge in wrong.

## *Flagrant Number*

The effect of lack heralded in a general sense of coin repeating
his flagrant things, his way of meaning disclosed all round some
inward manner, time bent to clear or press the spring and wait

not even an hour in a rattle of recall, so he heard himself felt, indeed
wasn't he only air and windows, emptier than the sea? Matter was
swallowed up near windows, raised at sight of work as it all might be.

Right relation nick the gasp of suddenness, make wings of going
with breath on force into the room. No stranger leap, his feet felt need
going, they said, above fact, so press air into any lapse of a moment,

air and so time as frame after the fact quite without casting back at
the plunge as figure of a father. Brush escape flood died under the
whole page, stirred air to the instant. Repetition of being heard even.

## *Least Ignorance*

A hung cause fell under matter for blood put to show
to be all recital of the house story, kept at last as guilt
put up in every civil name, enlarging a posture lapse.
Such a virtue flourish in any ground itself might rate a legend
as the swell of vision, as the next turn, as a full subject,
as even a purpose for his grasp of a handle broken off.

On your side, you gasp, they tell me, with blows patched
astray for a sight of difference and a signal of best scruple,
the only thing to like. I told about the wonder in time to
act it, left in miniature words, hard space of lips that fail
at each menace of elapsing artist flight, the gesture dropped
for the moment, the object seeking notice instead of beauty.

That instant remembered now in the secret tip, a hurry to
need nothing still might hang over a minute, close air to
refresh his hate of covers. Any test content ignored in
flushing tacit speech steps out of the article, with a lack of
level hands to humour me. Pocket impressions in edge words
swept away to take up matter to image what I want to say.

Make me care for tone trouble, the all round slip on scarce
distance, each space unspeakable, measured by charge that
both falls and cuts the act by presence denoted as close order.
Plunged in the chill passage with time for a rash effect of
words he had never heard, speech laid by in an inward gasp,
it came as an apparition, a lost tone in his ear spoke dream echoes.

In fact air at that pitch disposed in dark looseness might take
back all prime matter. Less time for world presence in that part
of the vagueness, so extend this figure and stroke memory of
the glimpse and act with style. Stamp under the rush to seek a
minute of full arrival. Nothing joined, sealed or fitted wings to
him. How had this voice just made his ear hold that sort of reserve?

## *Clear Nothing*

Pulled up before a form of honest person, all come
    to gape for profit fixed on signs of brute air on ground
        matter, a strain to make up the fold of surface breathing

To go out of being grasped, while he felt nothing for the time
    clothed and lapsing at a stroke of the door. Desire to this effect
        first fell on faint justice in the failure open to him to inspire.

He had dreamed of breath. A sacrifice of eye grace so manifest
    in a case of absolute alarm, windows bolted for this neat unknown
        at hand with a dull presence of material you couldn't begin to

represent or want such vibrated sense of measure. A flash of
    advance by real ceremony, the end minute was to be the least
        mark of stupid comfort, the force of being voiced and ordered.

## *Tight Orbits*

Silly desire for instant stress care pushed the will past any
ground of his feet so the word might be only measure
or manner formed like sense rising in arms and legs by resort
to vision, staring up his sleeve, to appeal for company as
shade breath on impressions of motion.

His words seemed to span your head trouble, still turned
back for quite due caution of addresss, the best spot on the
host body for form to invite a glimmer of wanting to be
intent on finding hard tact in speaking eye time if you care
more than nothing, mired in time to eat.

Say nothing apt to free a mite of frolic, a little left freshness
afraid of thought, in fear of power despite his figure of doubt.
Waiting must clearly do more to weigh things when the vexed
minute is a sense impulse letting it recognise an instant as
queer movement complication quite at ease.

Interfering time proved instant desire hindrance, a glimmer
to watch in air afterwards as well as to pick the same time
in any occasion to counter the other way in. Usher or
foreshadow power again by the tone as first despatched, sure
to share in words before time and intention.

Don't say I want out of the quick air of perception. Sense
happened to have to seem salient, showing vision losing
the stroke to act betrayal by tacit delay at home. Drudge at a
distance fit to toast the style of pain by the visit, making a
boast in time to mind the body to matter.

Patch over feet in time, save the present show to breathe
instant means in the measure of chill felt from talking about
being minded to figure a body lurking and wanting in time
by the nick of fear. Renewal of vision, the house in the lapse
already out with why the world looked ill.

Point instant fresh and own the rest to bear. Laugh to
see when to take another guess at time, answer free at once
in vital doubt of the same stroke of her eyes, inclined to
doubt dream abuse, this moment and time and sense and
no effect to intend a conscious want to touch.

## *Provoke Better*

Look sure for where he was and how it was in the eyes
nature had liked better, even for the minute. The house
might grow measured, a space apart against manner or
form in a glance at a shock he minded, confused for the time
as a wish to remember the matter of a laugh, wanting to
crop any instant harder. Stupid speech interest went on
to take in events by impulse as much as what you call captive
remark, in such things as eyes, matters he grasped away
in order of writing. Come to the window and suppose a
fresh mine of instant show to pocket the secret box, missing
with a certain pinch. His need to doubt every quiet inspiration
was now just passages with light on a slight letter protest
with art fashion success moment, the taste for matter
remembered in grace. The lapse admitted light renewals
to the room: it was before the pages haunted over this fact,
pen to the ear in right fusion from terms of further effect
denied later desire. Know the window as if in a play in your
absence, always to lose heart whenever you look over the
letter you lost and need, only an instant to ignore the taste
of restless time, not to avoid the act of direct flight from
art, wanting the troubled look as a sign to shut your eyes.

## *Defeated Scale*

Drop weight while facing the breath of practice reflected
        in tone less possible with the presence of
heavy reply saying so. It permitted nothing that would affect
        another world in this scarce snuffle any more
than a dream as light as need and control in fresh tribute to
        judge moments beyond the bristle of a step
to your eye distance for all time, to wink between the impulse
        and the matter in proportion to his figure of
the grasp of force, muffled or loose as the question of his
        words passing the window, silent and set to carry on.

## *Dark Otherwise*

Miss the account more civil for performed need
to leave credit, the utmost return to benefit in this
hand of information time checked with a language
to speak into my head. Even a minute bore the
worst look observed so that my name fits this
shrinking field of vision talked about as doubt or
virtue. Too much is quite enough, you wish to claim
work as disappointed rest, steps as some degree mine
to fall back on, a home for nothing less than gravity.

Miss the name of flush probability, miss right saying
appeal to doubt, but limit agreed matter in declared
lip pleasure, scarcely begun for wholly sharp relief
of circumstance. That instant force would be
apprehension, impatience for the moment to show
where I ought to desire to feel cut off in other words
for the absurd question of secret humiliation there
in a word uttered in the light, the answer to things
pledged to the old order, having to breathe so hard.

## *Doubtless Matter*

Apart still among the art of blankness with names for
a word to express being like nobody obliged to miss some
other creature then blaze out in time in the dreadful room,

trust your sudden effect more than that supreme exchange
of the impression of a force to oppose for a reason, look for
the key on a broken patch of much more than my words ask for.

I break with looking for the expected, at least as I have to let it hover
in a shade cast for a moment in its face, hide in air to recover
from that occasion to be the question I surprise as an image door.

To push open, I mean. Admire or follow, I am in the room.
Look at the end of time, beyond free speaking, spare that long
matter for a kind of threshold when I hold together and know that.

His fingers threw light into a justice interval to measure failure,
reading his speech rupture as some imitation of the crisis, his
care annihilated to chill dismay of stone, a drop of mortal instant.

The suspense thus attested seemed a hand at the door before
calling again for the pleasure of the last fancy years ago, eyes
as words in the mind, in fact pronounced as a glance of information.

The entrance, the stair: all made up in exchange, detached from
any step to the window with nature noted at the time by betrayal.
Some sense of right words for your cross ears, that was the tone.

The candid spasm of explanation here interposed as a sudden
response to personal discipline was to pile up her cell-effect
rigours to the open door to your time, never so much wanted.

Moments of constriction caught him in the act of inspiration,
a word trifle tightened by sharp spot warrant, without other tribute
to render about the turn in your house, letting that figure choose.

## *Strong Original*

Felt ruffle for quickness, the air taken from his world,
his mouth repeated sharpness as liberal array expression
at once denied even tragedy now, art supported by small matter,
the slope by his match open to bristle understanding how
this bridge to others' hands was altogether behind his back.
To flare apart a sign or blow breath in quick promise was
the site of an imagined voice applied with confidence at a
scene retention, a violation of the ear, unconscious in that
element felt in time with some organ, a shade of great words
that might continue telling parts of him to come out
as the phrase to glint and gather alarm deprived of action.

Impute impressions of relation to turn to the door, sense
before asking for your eye to judge almost a page even
to call most thought of hope to flower for credit time
by private instants, not many, drawn from want of other
light resources to put it in the sea by accident, hope warning
as chill promise suspended. In fact shadow appearance as a
step might touch awareness and measure the original reading.
Aim to just desire it as instinct of surrender to any air, still and
flagrant by presence, grin and be a momentary present by this
time without her occult cause of corrected fancy through the
strange stress this worst was the author of, held as caring.

## *Bedevilled Terms*

Grasp that moment, signal nothing for that light figure
and give a shade as a place free of vision, no pencil to note
or finish collections of neat caprice as soon as taste a fig or
mark your mind while I speak as I say, being so on the spot.

Where consciousness did grow up to the outer state, crude
symptom of some note of observation given for the fact of
exposure, these pressed each recognition of what surged up
as apprehension as if pursued by that glare, a disguise reflected.

A gasp for weight, transparent spots blur the light, walls in
the dark reach things and pinch matter even to face the idea
of balance, poor spark to complain of spirit shade and piece
words from the ground, the object world of broken touch.

Making that up, all names strike me as determined to be at
liberty with a hint of content desire moving to the sound of
parts of perception, scaring arrival in this grasp for an idea of
explaining a moment watching light flicker on wings again.

## *Actual Selection*

Take ten more to temper identification, use the name
of a house now the set penalties turn violent. So much left
to say the part after minding more than saying words
his mouth uttered, in a sense believing whatever words
were spoken before the public. That strange motive just
measured the moment, lost touch as words waiting for
people with an object, a sort of justice to believe in, as
eyes fail to think for the mind in the dark blue time that
grew, as his hand for an instant imputed to the sharpest
instant an expectation, watching. Wait and let it come,
tell me the place, darker and branching. Figure it out.
How had he said such waves of recall, left that word quite
as matter with a still reflection of these moments,
their searching light less attested and unexplained already.

## *Whirled Attention*

Reach through the question uttered without
moving to touch the wound seen by nothing
less than strange pressure from speaking it, as
the final twist between the house and the day

Matter into view, mutely next to this gift caught
close to tight mutual glare after the back of the
exchange measure. But eyes with anxiety, the
effect of words, mean to end moments of it all

The object in his sight has to glimmer at me
to affect you, catching it worse than free talk,
a bit afraid to be wishing to see friends in the
shade, dangling in the air, tracing the far range

Such a stir of suspicion, a plastic perch grasped
without moving in order to visit the house by speech
to the ear. You'd like the country, to leave there
tired of pretending to return the air in confidence

I come back from nothing down to a mention
in instant witness by blind pressure of doubt,
the rest of time even here for my own present
shadow, for the air I had taken for granted

Spot cast in light reflected in the known effect
blinked at a lost place in the world, in the room,
in the stress of being portended as if touch left
the very things we had shaken off repeated times.

# *Impression Really*

The trouble at the moment was not for the world
hurt, a dim drawing in instant thought like fear in
what he'd suffer in his answer to the idea of form,
but a second look out of the light of scrap earth we
all love. Don't change this show of touch, this figure
of dropped care in the tone of words as various desires
needed in order to arrange a common ground for
each to risk. Time to get more time wound up, wanting
to live half-prepared to agree more and be sad about
this growth of word trouble, renewed blankness as
the question of the break in the form of pitch and sound
in moments that glow to apprehend no answer to
brush away in knowing advantage, as he would.

## *Peep Contact*

Quickly as I told you the world let alone at last
seems to warn you to forswear your effort to act
upon wound up breath of inevitable forces and
carry off understanding in your hands, as if shade
was all edges for a moment, a prickly presence to fix
an instant with formless sound, unseen sense of
time struck silent. No one departed out of the
door, the open look at something that drove it in
by the ample house quitted by eyes and some sound.
Words without attention to the door at last addressed
the tone of renewed doubt, signs of measure as lack
of nearly nothing; the issue is thought in light and
proportion about conscious hours repeated as
perversity again, passing sharply after an instant
exposed to fear, to flutter more than his lips could tell.
Each well-kept approach would help free our exchange
of touch and find the world ready in divided awkwardness.

## *Earlier Pocket*

Quickly verified possession failed fingers or whatever shone without mine. How he held a mode of bright instant, a bovine air of physical breath, still drew the glare of contained eyes, another object, back to the door. The effect of his face hung on spoken views soundless for a time after the first jostle. Mute as to beg to make him appear at a sign intended to measure, wound up for something. Now this to reflect on presence and hours to swallow up in another sense. Aware of the rest, perhaps information after you see expressions like want and believe at a pitch that turned like touch in words—in their echo, he meant. If air was concentrated measure as a contrast to set in the house before we choose light, the idea might have been aware of the different recall haunted by conscious strain, a long time to be denied comfort and certitude. Most without being aware of a figure of imagination So few instants to match strange people. So you fail to discern the other note, the future of measure, the past of sense accumulations and continuities in time. At least add show as bewilderment meeting trouble as recent time unexpectedly hurt in its function, as if the same question was drawn to play off breath quite beyond light. Conceive any matter as a sort of injury appeal. Air felt still. Other things would be said, be published as an idea in time beyond any power of sense.

## *Sense According*

*A postscript*

A short street to get to material occupation, the door I groped for many years ago. Time before that account wanted to believe in the surface of my show, my final distress months' duration.

I dream or mean to be avoided in the process of this strange exhibition. Vividly to own all that interval lost in the past, saved in fear as the substance of waste words here. Uncanny desire.

Facts conceal it, material like consciousness of this question in circles arranged in air in glimmers of economies of sense. I just nail things to catch this dictation, an accident floats in my head.

The moment taken over to this wavering margin to speak of living in this sense of divination, to own the ground portent, work the world loose from the air in the house, sprawl in the evoked aspect,

Come near the matter in tone. What I want is to grasp each nail by betrayal of the terms of catastrophe, collapsing the ground in this modern measure. It may help to keep the question in so many words.

My free hand requires pages of flesh, a kind of literal mind. Nothing extracted in a message to you, resting eyes on the house as the balance between two to speak a word of what I mean not to say, a note in advance.

# A SPACE BASED ON HEARSAY

## *Air Flitter*

Binding light over the brow thrown from the air soft
matter incapable of rhetoric assuming status attention,
with so true an eye to extract value out of our reach, why
mean to explain such posh dismal magic as fictional wish?

Fly over the wall wearing a show made good in another
language, press a petal to rags to doubt about moving out
of time as a scene offers to flutter the tongue and grove
and flood the whole array with pastoral multiplex parody.

Begin inset reason of shadow rakes to recognize the
moulded conflict he or she brings by the yard to music. It
is not necessary to explain four words as a form left behind
in a seclusion that works with silence or an Aeolian harp.

Abiding in their back yard containing the words called art
of losing, it's still there in the sense of a glimmer impulse line
cut back at the end, as burnt lists shake against the cold mind
on implied stress, like a mouth blight still without rhythm.

Stuck material points well up and go back as what follows
from an email dream first without shouting so much in bed.
Time on concrete sift to brief air ruin. Notice a message as it
stands for everyday models of relief in the mouth or body.

Spice this object in abject damage space to a yard of void sense
marked out in unhinged tenses, a way to consume that thought
understood as a sight no longer missing an origin sensed about
the wings of matter as they fade over and over into air flitter.

## *Gloomy Clamber*

Exotic narrative city to malign each day permitted stop and search side street caginess or brim aware through the gates least aperture soon told while strolling back all fearful for flight steps back down midsummer ratchet shift for some ancestral theory of struggle. Dog remedy fails under the sun, falls again. Zoom contact page scroll, chestnuts and acacias a partial antidote outside this approach to plain stories or lives. String out getting shot of it all, alley between variables endemic to wider issues, cycling beside the canal. Repose in the letter, money to efface the destructive movement a mere abstraction. Stop-gaps concede a cloud of oblivion in common time, walkable traces leading to emergence of fingertip dislike, even hate. To what purpose all this bird twitter chat scrabble in bramble tangle nobody can say, throats constrict at the thought of such lucidity, bare as poles as far from innocent we glance at black maps, all inert, s-shaped and unconsulted in this feverish puzzle.

## *Exceed Frame Time*

Greeting studded internet predictions
burst through glint, left now only like
sun squalls, with core time building up
on the edge bent a little defaulted to
late snow on the sea, up from the drone.
My first number shrug happened too
far out to deal with, say a car left
by the quarry for a voice call, take charge
of some ancient bucket, look away or
strain fate by crane to another place.

Plate glass closure, savage tray put down,
no rubber bands, no screwdrivers, a copy
of the spirit, some flying creature at last
filling part of the air, lost to sight. Numb
race to violent counter answer explicit and
essential fittingly. Not failed, comrades,
save the material world, the chest freezer
heritage boutique guilt store. Rinsed under
clouds, touch flaking to reveal an absence
of what was imagined as assemblages.

That nail connects light to bramble, keeps
anxiety cobbled to one hand, a field of
force full of density if you squint a bit
to mint focus adjusted for hawthorns and
ash. Hinge tremors return unsaid each night
begun in speeded-up promises, just you
wait and see. Least shed, pelt freely. Hear
today this morbid outcome broadcast,
rain forecast to slope in between scales
taken up quite cold and not itself shared ever.

## *Get an Ear Test*

Guess with submerged forms to attend
to, note some goal constructs in the concept
here supplied with time off limits to turn
clear back. Each look for later hover
flies, raked lavender, told about it, known
to be false as a kind of opposite to need
the earliest threat to earth you remember,
now all this and its dead eyes lurking as a
special undergrowth offer you can't refuse
or know about, perky intrusive hazels. Get
over here, feign colour for foreign shapes,
think licorice touches recombined in sphere
manifolds no questions asked. Thistle and
goat's beard allow a pause. So call it music.

## *Potentially Permanent*

Parallels speak further things, the weather itself
to give support status leaks over high ground in
this wider sense, action or reading as an opaque
fabric, a veil against any ephemeral perception.

Total balance averse, muffle decoys conspire to
never end or stumble as one might too easily yet
carry on to doubt embodied plunges, safe from
this rough story as it falls in words that flap about.

Who needs subject form in closed aspect or in a
wider memory process usually well filled by rakish
nature enduring distant interests, no plot winding
a puppet fantasy of public life in draft wish code?

Just hand the desire and fill out the normal case
present tense state, cloud ahead and visions inscribed
from green pages in the mouth. A title word hangs
unspoken, a circling buzzard its bogus parallel.

Oh no, no buffer grinding. Earth heave butterfly
fear, bottle tremor translated to the clouds as innuendo,
spreading shadow to remain a lot of stuff, words
crammed in the photograph crawling like repro ants.

Yellowhammer rustle in the flash ear, carbon lost out
in the air, vagrant beings the mock shadow stretches
like a manifesto focus grin across the grass all aflutter,
a poor bubble of the inner self we never close now.

## *Please Call Us*

Knot some broken focus quite up tight
as bees rise and fall by the dream outfall,
unable to be marked as frank attention to
an imprint secretly with a pollen ring
panic regarding some tumult of sublime
memorial shining over voices muttering
behind fountains. Stillness leaves.

It left, civic pride left in a way that reused that
frame, this web, to set more air into the space
above literal sense in years to come, to puff
up custodians of ordinary personal problems
and manage further discourse for cash. Grass
matted, autumn crocus glowing at the edge
half-grasped thoughts shaped by waking.

The ring panic never left, sea-level clout dis-
placement amounting in practice to an island
of waste in a sea of waste. Nobody answers
the hunger tangle calling by day in choked
shivers of warp enigma. A sort of quietness
arrives like menace or footsteps and stays.

## *Why Call it Again?*

It went against the glass, anything but
compressed life face to the green ones
lacking a far cooler origin, with intended
motifs as rapturous machine objects. We
invent chaotic bias in order to see the
contours' maximum energy impacted—
or worse, not afraid of the past, abstract
and close to lyrical incessant gusto. There's
no reason to call it anything else now, just
call it by its name. Its name against yours,
filmy hopes message syndrome spot cash
reality drawn to owl noises through the
darkness, what more can I say? Almost
placid again, reflect on it, reflect it back.

# *Only Displacement*

Supposed to possess drafts for when I started
those neglected words about what visual trial
might last a life in the version cut for time, a
few chosen sentences in an array of radiant
tumult, enough to compose an oblique speed
present, scraped away, seeing things dying, what
urban beings keep in mind as ambiguity, it might
be in order to point a brief new shaping fiction.

Cue sparks, closed footpaths, assumed creed
departed as rain falls steadily over the abyme, a
cascade some time ago seeded to seem now not
remembered, immune to habitat missing the light
to boost each lurch to name text's spurious smile,
eroding slowly to act as a type of abandoned gradient
by sad experience wise and fluttering diction
speaking honey near hope to filaments imparted.

This was imagined. Or at least an attempt to read
through the fissures of a voice to get behind the dial
and into the works, to see how there might be arcadian
observations in sudden flights above the trees, friction
between concepts, black versions nestling towards night
and the barn-owl sailing towards me. Always a climb, a
dying ash back by that hedge, hips and sloes got
in heavy weather up there to wet the lake as birds darted.

Some kind of fiction then. Clouded air for a while
puffing thought stuff into old frames, like the tradition
of dead generations caressing the eye and backing in fright
from the daylight as woods decay and call faint-hearted
feeble cries to the slipshod act of model camera shot.
All go on ruined each from far to sell from hand to crime, a
loss to us alas in adverts for the last chapters, with obedient
elders smiling in deleted expectation of a right to need.

## *Past Taste*

Respond by larks hum kindly light
        tasting of dropped vanilla in a hybrid
field placed to one side fixed into this
        attempt to reveal communal minds
to describe really ignorant bubbles
        of each perception to surmount
a stroll through the forest within
        as for instance friends clearing
access to concept functions and points
        that would be free and unbounded
approaches to vision enfolded in
        radio waves in spite of space rashly
kind woven through lasting signs
        unsounding between each and
over e.g. a cat mutual-hearing humans
        from windows posed to provide
instance in essential vision charting
        complex far experience manifest
and nettled by unseen bunting chats
        once lost from memory as proper
calls reply from twig rebates and must
        deepen to remain caught in time

## *Leaving No Trace*

This spiral prank a collared dove's slight twitch
lost a last twig now hold fast a challenge in hand
to calibrate brash earth so easily lost to pointless
fiction permanent hurt twizzle uncaptured daily

Writers blind as possible disabuse in language
behind the voice solid sound opening to cliché
moments of partial meat around lace obsession
over wallpaper stubs that appear back at the tether

Of wood-tongue slipway refusal long in reverse
even so, and recently driven off that piece of land
leaving what goes real to speak of paradise or
some woodland grudge posture claiming the right

To it. Little meaning of their own dogs what they
think they say, disarray in the ear if it fails to cosset
our long wake sense as after supper defiance breath
shapes what leaves nothing but a footprint everywhere

## *Of Denser Things*

It was the latch to an extent not shadowed now
 gelid light valley leaves moss and lichen reticent
a ravenous montage echo ritual, food for pattern
 recognition software in hands growing up against
parallel future circumstance caved in for partial
 smudged windows down two points on human life.
Left out stacks observe banded material walls
 wood strips imagined desires the implausible view
bound in compass flash full screen tongs as if only
 current hopeful appetite would shun such solidity,
a norm-busting moment of death-watch artery in
 vetiver image translation reproachful. Gasp impulse
radical to gnarled film gesticulation memory shivering
 then suffering made up of tracts of threat thread
to shift what satisfaction might engorge the present day
 after day, its steamy edges blue sticky and intolerable.

# IMAGINARY SKY

*The Woods, where Beasts, or herded Men abide,*
*As thick are planted there, and near their side*
*Fantastick People too, in false Fields move,*
*And Fowl, in larger Fields of Aire above;*
*Swift, as the winged Thought, that feigns their flight,*
*Yet never soaring out of inward Sight;*
*Though with their fancied Wings, they higher flie,*
*And traverse all th' imaginary Sky.*
— Richard Leigh

## *A Hasty Dip*

Half belonging to this regard a hasty dip
may be its final nicest question to do
out the way like a room for the walls
at midsummer, from the first comfort
kept to lose and then you have even
this dry view with the lapse of years.

Darker shades of some head invited
for colour, a fresh alarm pitch for an
elastic interval message, a warning
emphasis right through the first hour
of omission. Turning in a moment
in his private circle, asked to mark it

as apt and weak like an old story
made violently new, all done up to remain
a subject loosely doubtless in measure.
In a fine fact of exposure motive haste
he struck her as sign, as degree, call it
nothing uttered, not even a word subject.

We've just managed to say nothing of
the short wave tension rather lighted up
from China and wired to the line. No
lines conscious of poor scribble for a man
she held exposed to allusion but nothing
was as it was once begun, my finger on the bounds.

So of dreams when traces stab at a figure
I sing. I begin from behind my head
with a blot to trample as my head feeds me
and climbs my stick collage with all the art
in the world exercising obstacles as a child
would have been its customer or eaten it all up.

## *What Ever Next?*

It was about context responsibility first
written in the difficult motif of a class and
signalling at the outset none of its value
had to be axed to document the virus poll.

What were these birds? Lost from vineyards
lost from spindle lost from the map of music
day to day to prompt us depleted to eat
what we hear as silence pleated in the ear

and create islands of smirched glass etching
them instead, scorched years of blasting to
fetch in the last remnants ever told or drilled
to buggery short-term and strictly off the books.

Welcome galanthus glimpses lighten to redeem
what nothing else for it lost to dark or troubled
hand to collar drove wrongs collected red bar to
press or expected proposals pushing up through.

Snow drops from the cloud formula unfurl in
masks as streetwise shingle hives a loud melancholy
raw air played thin on distant wires single sweet
noises dire warnings to range away in order

to continue the soundings beyond mountains.
The detained miles lucent merge in memory
from moth clutter to spam fritter grim pastures
and impostures all lost as remnants of old music are.

Stitch to hamper a blue button, expect to use its
register in wild drugget underfoot meshwork
if only once or twice with eyes fresh and open
wide, ladder back balanced by twigs as if to say

most words deliquesce here in the wood's raw
gains. Barge telepathy less strongly flows to
plug the gap variant trend in material impact
per capita, notably in income, now wide garble.

Where the ever more sublime fumarole gasps
interrupt word thought expressed as pierrot sigh,
what remains of all the salient world so girt
with wrong brash twirling tweets against us?

Look now, a green fireplace addressed as change
trading notes in pleasant components scratched a
kind of theatre of chance in work known to make
chores for thumb or teeth in a lost projected refuge.

In the mid smile switch off a magnetic vocal
fox in casual decades of woodland out of choice
used precarious cheap song panic, some club in a
blind rule category noted all right to darkness.

People call it a wren habit spelling 'foredoomed'
and bent on obsolete classic survival power, far
down by yon bewilderment, aback if you peer
more dimly towards the old place of a morning.

But what other thing follows next was written
only for several days, stirred up the wretched past
of no importance. To meet allusion did one good
and paid no attention to whatever it might have been.

# *Another Subject Incline*

Against a landscape, sleep will convey
doors disputed in excess flow and speak
the place it has to determine or negate.

Image limits can stand ego springs to
arise in never-ending limp plays from the
zone of warmer days obligingly in another

matter of course, in a dismal mask followed
at sense pace in fused edges slipped up
twixt cup and mix-up plunged in our plight.

Stripped down kind of eye sedge puffing
up to incline again for weeping as it leads
to give mind its oily draft surface by the marsh,

inclined to wander claim to slash enlisted
process skein by cloud shapes by skin lucky
sleeping vellum bound to settle a tune.

Or steal one from the tune orchard, panic
rummage too much for a refuge in stupid
heat, a key in a door too much for a voice

to invent or sing to envelope everything
in a cloud of ongoing superfluous sense,
words summoned to contradict all music.

## *Infernal Duo*

Where in all this listed detachment of human
diversity and stake problems is a cause of fear
cloaked by a final offshoot of inverse time? If
the book collapses in so short a period, do they
attend my best mind printed or claim total
fairness? The centre is left out, turned down
from the angle of this war as they did with every
irony in his flat. It became a fashion like the
phonology of wallpaper, a song of salvation
whispered in places apart, evidence even of
resistance to something in the air, nothing to
get hold of except that earworm and a voice
trying to tell you it was scripted to live through
it again and again. Only be told the best, it said.

## *Radish Nostalgia*

Or banish unofficial rose disguise that
blows up time immemorial a gorge to
hanker after. This afternoon my prism
for cloudy climbs, my cover story now
basically rounded with superimposed
marginal teeth in self defence. Half eaten
I dream.
                                        Red posters up
at corners I began reading again between
a line not crossed, an eye not doubted
as stonecrop and hawkbit crop and bite
and grow. Jackdaws all day here. Let
them come they will.
                                        Profusion atone
and bless each reticule kitchen, tender
refusal fine birth for supper glimpses
ever open utter blending hero reduction!
Might also drips. As night devours the car.
Whose lips are right or often say they are.

## *Lemon Sole*

At first glance the edge sign tempts
to that code below we now find so
fond of so little, nothing about coffee
to go out of date except this danger of
the edge of things so to be overlooked.
Tap fear entry beyond the scope of
this key absent at flowing time don't
you see what I mean, hooked they can
be simple uncomfortable thoughts or
be hand in club twitching under a table
set for three or more. Wood pigeon
trunk calls charred wire woodcut to
fix up and running a sort of ladder to
betterment set with my own hands. Eat.

## *I'm Not Sure*

What critical vice you are told to keep
it lost a roar over shell sand to zip it
in the mind's eye stalkless and invented
to peer out of places. Gaze steady
across the field, flax in flower as
witness some sprig character burdock
lens for a missed wave, mollify the
flinty surface ordeal over paper, over
what's buried in case of rain not forecast,
over the not known. A service tree as
a surprise by the field margin. The owl
in my heart flies like the hole in my art,
bent blunt by hedgerow, lunette relief
filling memory with its borrowed arch.

## *All Mere Use*

Exiled from the top box viewed from the edge of
some lakeside ground it misled grim supporters no
longer accidental shadows marching along the way.

At least he said it in a language where home was a time
of day or a return ticket, crossing the border as it does
to settle outside any event or thought quite recklessly

adjusting is true of fronts anyway, apostate worries
to sleep on weld or frown over musk mallow light dream
tread. Where will you put yourself when night will fall?

A value circuit then. Quite useful and extensive from day
to day it falls short or we do move beyond the scope
of the view which they say will be gone before flowering.

## *Wilding Paper*

Another bee out of sorts on the foxglove
on the way to peace after tea with all that
bent for chicanery filling every crevice untold
unfolding a thing twice bales of hay today

argued against marginal use or glued new
mulberry chromosome failure overhead
for a rainy day brink to skate on the surface
secretly rating a foundation for military harm

considered account settled as grave dispatch
real figures even poets might flinch at the desert
air suddenly in every issue shaped migration
before brush touches paper, the breath of bark

itself put to invisible use in violent ink
poppy scatter already done so by the log in
time they are fledged and lodge elsewhere
chaffinches and suchlike with their own ethics.

## *Imported Raw*

Part of the conversation against it those branches could be
learnt when they would have his hands over the sun out of the
window flat and wide weighing like the sky imagined in empty
talk for a time, still asleep or half awake and exposed to drive
away how they would be, glint lost in the mist. Reason copied
out in mutual aid before prohibited sweet thought, all they wanted
dropping like flies, liberated unease to proliferate an action *fixe*
often at a true found output traded off and attacked into safer
years later in the century maybe. Dressed up at all levels, dew
so small a distraction agency with a view device hosted by door
frame lighting, all visible to forget their slow emergence to
forge immersion in landscape deceit with dull nightingales—
isn't it great? Smoother paper display clusters coming into flower
as raw material as silence rolls and rolls on as long as it takes.

# UNCOLLECTED POEMS

## *Some Constants*

*for Elaine Randell*

that shining yellow field
alternating current
a waterfall of objects
chests-of-drawers and pens, brushes
the sweep of an arm
A Man Called Spade
the love of space
we find in a knowledge of
nourishment
and its place in our lives
in parenthesis
where it belongs
in the rain, Can you forgive her?
the spirit, the finger, the wings
you fold a fine energy
lining the moment with
a test of poetry
and it passes
is carried shoulder high
silent behind glass
glass that dissolves
you know it is made of sand
and trickles through the glass
moment by moment loved and loved
the land's end
in the eye of a needle
never now later when
the time is opaque as
a michaelmas moon and lights
more than the room's moment
in a shining yellow field

(published in *Saintly Fingers* 4,
edited by Brian Marley, December 1975)

## *Herman, what makes you tick?*

a common language or code
not a common set rather a common set
of that text, a shared form, a side street
a residue of earlier days
a libidinal investment, the photographic present
rises when we are called upon
on wings the optical illusion of thought
only & hovers predatory
obliged to borrow trappings
for the denial in his mouth
composed entirely of dots
like his disintegrating face
and hard beak set in the middle of it
disguised as an official position
which remains but does not mean

the positions of such reactionary authors
may be considered surface phenomena, rationalization
and disguises for some more basic source of energy
of which they are unaware

le monde rentre dans un sac...
Is this the completion of the thoughts of the past?

(published in *Saintly Fingers* 4,
edited by Brian Marley, December 1975)

# *pourquoi chercher le bout de la chaîne qui nous relie à la chaîne?*

bones stick out where a strand of wool
has frayed the pattern of knowledge
every moment every look
is consciousness inhaling singularity

directing itself through intelligence
out to other things
inhaling and exhaling
all of nature's energies

gleanings of night draw back
like snails the onslaught of postures
a newspaper at breakfast
twisting the social heart

across the face of actual man
where are his feet?
what is the solid ground?
say what you want is impossible

words belong in the street
as they live in the day
the orange flies up
to the ready hand that grasps it

I have no facts to offer
as light labour or love
these constants smoulder
and the fire moves on

(published in *One* 3,
edited by David Chaloner, Spring 1976)

## *Happy Endings*

*for Tom Raworth*

No other way this
cathedral in the pools
annuls everything
in shadow interrupts
the middle of memory
it was somebody

Pure water image
of precious stones
leaving wings
broken flower
crushed in your ear
against the quay
for ever impossible
body would recover
until those words

Door to
your place
swallows shadows
gathered in
vents only the trees
in front of my
eyes when I
come back
progress from a
distance plays
sad truth tunes

Just as you are
dying a marble corridor
shining grooves
water on chests
alone harbours a cry
sonorous shade
you might say
danger no longer
protects you

Competition breaks
water morning is really
a speed of red
to dust your solitude
motionless breath
further than the breeze
clocks some body
then dust settles
again doesn't exist
out of mist
work also remains
a silence louder
than a sound
now continues begins

## *Ideal Fingers*

Wrongs and rocks and masses
and other nations on horizons
attached to their masters by seaside
healthy ties whittled free of danger
appear to be rock pools
or ammonites or caves full of sand,

A view to be carried further
harassed by a citizen to look down on
all directed to the inside
cliffs of fall or whatnot, take a picnic
or just go into a country. The great outside.
Dark sky, strath, calm wave

Vexed into whirlpools by selling short
evening on the rocks or darker
there now as resilience cracks appear
crumbles Lyme Regis bones or gathered
thrift from cliffs through the wide City
near unimagined chasms and died.

Until the dawn light running
over sand, plastic bottles, seaweed, waste
plonked down, cleaned for nothing
composes a view, derives a prospect,
the sea far out and quiet and the sun
rising to display profusion of discourse.

Money shall be the willow, pollarded
as fiends pursued them there on
Channel 4 News, snow relentless

except on sand deep as the air
as mountains split and mortgaged
as you stand on chalk and breathe heavily.

Precarious outlook, high impact
basalt rock and old mines
topsy fiscal laggard pouring capital
great stones against the ragged cloud
over Kinder roll back and praise
the work of English nature futures.

Hold steady. I know the image
in the light of day or like the sea
and its rapid spells of land, upland,
headland and vantage point where
eyes and minds in strange embraces
plough the barren waves night and day.

## *60 Windows*

*for Jenny Diski*

Tiny room whose window was never opened
Curtain for the window
On the cane chair under the window

*

Pale green even in the window
Emptying the basin out of the window
Halts by the window and gazes

*

Lay on the ground under the window
Kneeling up to the window
An octagonal vaulted chamber with a balconied window

*

Her bed had its back to the window
Through the curtainless window day stole in
She went to the other window

*

Sitting at the table near the window, working
Opened windows into the wrong world
A gale, exploding against the window

*

Awnings lowered outside the windows
A reproduction of a stained-glass-window angel
Whistling up at vague windows

*

Got up and went to the window. It was raining again.
Early light, coming through the uncurtained window
With its tiny windows looking on to the street

*

Pat wandered from the window and took up the George Moore novel
He came out through the French windows
She got up and stood at the window

*

There was moonlight in the window
There's a sharp rapping at the window
I am in the window, smoking

*

They had seen it happen from a window
Then went to the window that looked on the street below
Watching you from the apartment window

*

In my memory, at the window
The rain was still thudding against the window-pane
I think that I might open the window

*

A camera is being held to the window
Silver things in the window
From the street the windows were in darkness

*

His reflection could be seen in the front window
High up, from one of the small barred windows
His right arm through the open window

*

I put all the lamps on and opened all the windows
A huge wall broken by gaping windows loomed above
Sordid glare of shop windows, made beautiful by distance

*

A board nailed across a broken window
They opened all the windows
Sat and sewed by the window in the clear autumn afternoon

*

The room was almost in darkness, the windows quite covered
The night I stared at from my window
A castle whose windows were glittering orange squares

*

The windows, between lengths of white embossed satin
Our windows, on the second floor, overlooked the street
The butcher pulled down black window shades

*

She had been sitting in her own window
The inner courtyard on to which my window looked out
The middle one of the three windows was half way open

*

The sun filtered through the windows with remarkable subtlety
Rushed to the window, not to sail out of it
No lights behind its white painted windows

*

Has to look out of the window at the elements, at nature
Draw down the upper frame of the window
The windows were shuttered. But there was a crack.

*

*60 WINDOWS is composed entirely of phrases that mention windows, taken from page 60 of 60 different novels. It was written to celebrate Jenny Diski's sixtieth birthday.*

## *For John James*

It's very important
to make your lines
and stick to them
remembering their names

unless you're as empty
as a wind-swept fen
with a thought in your heart
that sounds like a line of John James

## *Poem for Numbers*

They fold into themselves turn
to such days seen in what follows
as my feelings to your ten cares
quite badly and funny and dry

show him how
angel of words
about not being
so many things

madly writing to the long sob
of fatal haunts and boiled chicken
to flap the biggest shape
in an identity parade

how far I am without so much
as French closing as it touched
a mark to count on the tongue
left to ourselves at vespers

as they said this copy is
for me, a masterpiece of mind
whispers in my ear in the manner
of a split minute to you

if they add up, a word of morning
a far place on my fingers
you know I'll be about to pour
the floods of our life

on to the word sky
an impulse to talk
voices into figures
to measure ourselves

# *Iron Letters*

## I

Utter received
& savage verse
streaming in
once written
told as much
as ever breathed
I was in the sea
but will be too
much more than life
the greatest anxiety
quite in itself
in letters
nor desire no
phrases nearer
than it show any
balance in
your hands
writing neglect
the flames I have
no claims to be
prose not yet finished
as you meditate
sheets of a life
and afterwards
tell my remaining rags

## II

Suspect of the senses
you wish to make up
felicity and a song
to lose the bond

silly blind and then
can't glimpse fire
by an overturn
say nothing say put

from suspense
between the lines what
naturally wishes human
being so quietly

for some stage
so stays by that
time so no time
was lost in the age

abide by his pains
like the milky way
vicinity and access
green fruit in autumn

## III

Slacking paces the way
scribbling caused
opening a drawer

look towards the sofa
better to forget
whoever's work that was

reflections come too
but never the outcome
gives me any pleasure

merely personal
write to them and assure
my books not my power

to promise at four o'clock
answer to remember
what to say nothing about

people in a garden
tell me they do here
they have and keep furnished

## IV

He is abated as
calamities with rose
a long time
know how order
let out of your hands
to any concerns
trust in it seems *just*
in July ears
my name will be
in disorder to raise
the *father* and severe
in a rainy morning
sticks waiting
for us immortal
inside and out
owing to the heat so
disagreeable as I choose
my *serious* advertisement
or some town on your coast
transmuted subject
but to tell you this
the worse it seems
believe me

## V

I say what he means
but wish to refuse both
the issue of it
to the usual possession
and, to change the subject,
are you in England?
menacing this cold slab
of visit to any part or parts
insisted and detained
my improper valise
I have suspected certain
outward signs do not
suit me in such a state
torn and missing, degraded
or weak from ways of thought
for whom I have given up
my own scenes without my
saying any more
even in appearances
with a chair or table and
the blindness of beginning

## VI

Was it kept by your translation
till you can clear the house
to plague you with the burden
of the theatre of knots?

I will come to any place
one way or another:
in the eyes of the free world
he *wished* to have an end in view

do you want me to find
probable good cause?
I shall require politics to think
but first, a word while

letters came to correct me
in this country still more
public and astray to share
against the field of the knife

for they are not popular
released "to confess"
and creep by last post
variations on mask in the flesh

from a print of a word
all mixed over overturns
say it soon, warn me quietly
and I will go on like printing

## VII

No harm done to know you
waxed spelling like "laugh"
alone and act from any tight
rounds on the death of my fee
at burning matters and bones
of foggy morning with violets
two or three very gladly sent you
and many trials and conclusions
which perhaps you know better
as a certain solace in small writing
more quietly swept down
with part of mankind
with funds down under my days
about to begin with youth, beauty
and the paper diamonds reproached
like war, my friendship arrested
and deceived for the liberties in my land!
Does this deserve the name who not
only is torn and the rest
in such a moment I have lived
*for you* with the thought of this hardly
pleasant nor eloquent unalterable portal?

## VIII

Your bureau and doors to perpetual
suspicion and the house clear and
so very like your writing a tragedy
in black and white and some
shuffles as I am now his dancing
beat. They love us. It wears nothing
not because he keeps the difference
sold from a letter, continuing earth
not to sell out with my terms, nor my
people of suspense. You never name her
or scrape to go on in a solitary forest
to prove all sides in a green bag
no matter flit out of it but recollect
we wait while seeing it was written
in impartial decree which can only restore
melancholy testimony to an unknown person

## *Coda*

Mind to read between
what I have written to the Wind
in fragments of proper hours
in every sense what it wants
has been hit on the style
but no fine phrases for you to read

# *Wyatt's Voices*

## I

The cover felt like a homage between the landscape of docks, a breakfast shift by the bicycle shed that ignored a collapse outward before climate change had a plan using reclaimed bricks shrunk to the visitor it might have been. This is not built of active cells, it ties explicitly rhythmic light to opening the space that dreams it in place of matter, not of the term's displaced opacity, an opaque capacity from the ideal earth to flounder in the thread we are calling the act itself built from the edge of blank stones at the top. Big sacks outright baked surfaces in a room somewhere in between. Matter tends a stance letting go the letter developed in the work, four words that must be said inside through a visible stone water level doing what they do best like me in metal, hearing the news. The surface speaks because of credit in time with greyscale unease.

## II

Referred back desires were discussed in a familiar glow until guilty things and rash disguises did for his own betrayal in ruins by set forms carried out by turns on top of it. Dumped by and large under the spell of time to time to no avail, and sheathed in a sense of bright red lives locked into the flat, still ruins conveyed a cool field of banal elements rather than what lies within a vast equivalent. What sustains. To do this but to be in a play so as to make it the way it is lit up in its own way, which had been a kind of speech defect I suppose. Nothing eludes rhyme very fluid and implicitly forming a temporary address as it will be still my lot before I'm done. Now bar a few to drop left in white lick it's all empty in the century and better than ever except for the stones, drowned again, not even turning his head at the sound of such cries of pain and such dying human gleams of light so wanted and so yet not for you at all, not ever.

## III

What surfaces is something to seize well. An object not
obscured can be called and will carry the impression of a
labyrinth like the pool's surface silent to prevent disorder.
Call it friendship like music or like a field of pitch marks
overlaid with pale ochre streaks in a point of view. Rueful
and falling low the curve of the light streaked with grey feeling
to be not so much fallen back as snatched to the surface
of things on the grass with silvery trails as you stand by the open
window marked and wan. East and west they run from each
other as absence leans against the door-post or clings between
things like different readings devoid of edges and almost remote
thin layers of being laid bare emerge at each floor only with
white skin and footprints set taut or hollowed out on the other
hand profoundly. Green stone honed to the same staggered horizon.

## IV

Roses like ice on the common tongue, cries arose on the mouth
of deep hedgerows fluttering in alarm at the dark hollow so
sung down the ages in bright tones charged with forgetfulness
at the heart, a cascade of petals as you put it into words again today.
And I remain constructed out of ruins, dark matter with surface
glazing mixed media shaping words in readiness to fly up
like a sparrow in the brambles to a nest or to the nets of the heart's
forest half-choked with honeysuckle and fragrant with more roses.
What now indeed sets up is all to know the knot which first
failed the past, warped how the house was a few lines last autumn
behind the rain, made it solid now like this piled on tables condensed
from the seconds by a wasp. Light implacable broke the fire
in the heart and gripped the face, a dense blue sea to be pinned
down to nothing in hand like the outside of words in the darkness.

## V

Now stand as an aspect of modern life to rove around visible
but lost till dusk trails into flames that flutter and vanish
into the waste of time, blood on the cut paper put to use
by the work. Feed on clouds and echoes unset like a patient
evening an austere wink among the nets developed and fixed
as private as lives, loose ends scrabbled in the bush played out in
posturing claims about home. Right to land or left at sea. A heap
of broken images in each version we all dream as raw film dreaming
of the house, material from the first attitude like whims on the move.
Torn in strips with the sea glimpsed through burned earth never to
speak of it as a child might fear to see it there wrinkled and green
yellow and bleached of light — it is the world it does not care to
see us go into the streets like a sail. Where it rose is waste, a cloud
of dark insects rising about the bank, the sound of new barbed wire.

## VI

At all hours under the direct address something will still move
if you want pain sharpened after a cab to an amused arch and implied
result most of the way by the symbolic burning. A rebuff even.
I believe it can be more than it is to miss their purpose disguised
in fantasy and the earth. A certain aim holds the lines and now
the shades of moral stable life fade. How no doubt he did side
with a brother after this trumpet of no good forms for a story. A storm
would be unlikely. Faked persons infest the place as a black page and
now fast. A neat row of trees dished up in returning discord tagged
or felling and last to go over before the skies are fenced in with
spite. Colloquial French pulled from the water at hip height to
flash out of it turned to the act cut in wood, one edge alone. If you
don't want the sighs of woeful hearts or scruples like five crows in a
lyrical passage remember why time and again is used a good deal
more often than I'm ever likely to say.

## VII

Dance the day in the spirit of its end before ever again
in the best love of contraries in the heart of this time of
stone. The cosmos gleam by dahlias, the goldfinches scatter,
wet grass underfoot, it all adapts easily to my way of
thinking shaped as unmistakable light. Do you take this
and will you, whispers and declarations like a voluntary trumpet
hold the afternoon and have and comfort still. Chance may
not be so primed with the mark of ascension, a door with
three steps incomplete to the entity late in life, the simplest
of human plants. Towards you. To you. As the mist clears
I form different habits we could start by saying everywhere
in my thinking but who is to say that the occasion is not a new
form we expect to think. A blackcap was singing the whole
piece in a music of love made up of notes of which this is one.

## VIII

If what can stop is doors as one or two have made the clip
to mark unfinished acts for the use of things not noticed
day by day, the irons there in his strange fiction they simply
closed down. Why what voices not even loud they lobby
they run they stand around they spill small bits of language
from the age of self to my thought harbour. Unhappy bones
stretch skin envelopes too tight in pride or vanity so to this
do relief heels clicking neatly on the wood all too buff and
leathery for a medium so be carried off and on. Pick up the tray
to prime the bar before it comes down steel again on steel mind
your fingers wipe that smile off the floor as chill gulls swoop
over wet concrete beyond this view of things. Most change no
more but your own firm cover in this hot wet air out of service
just out of it time out of mind out of the kindness of your heart.

## IX

Even when could place run out her own kind under these jobs
and see a way out early? To think by far beloved paths deep in
hand in the germ of this still free to say embers, still forms on
paper that hover over this theatre without a word circled in ink,
nothing left to hear out there. Cup sandy bounce up into blue
light to fly on meat with such a voice or table dream to leap into
the fire, a night of burns in store stove in like a dream to turn to
deadly pain. As to be heard where I have waves under that loot
a sound of words again graven in radio marble, the grace of airs
itself not for resale, left on earth by dint of seasonal wax damage
in bits of peace now lost. How to signal mine once set as I do wake
too soon to steady rain? All in mushy mess and trodden into grass.
No cure glows anywhere except to my ear so much bent by all this
bridge-work. Dial hectic change, time waves, cold grey stones, oh well.

X

At any event timed sweet showers becoming short to your room to farm or book and rest easy by dialling our agents adjacent to the truest life are now all stations gone. It's no good clipping the view in the high resolution evening light in some ruthless turtle cut, it's just like another doll's house down on the trees. Grid thought on Sunday morning, clouds to give interest, resting eyes tracking inward to more waxy dreams of colder air. Lairs of code keep readings in a secret place of softer cotton or debilitating noise. I didn't see the point of another trumpet anyway given the pile of books we have to deal with. Hurt feelings make histories from below from under the skin's transit dust from curves of syntax. That's just between you and me as you take your fingers out of your ears. No chance of rain now, doors to the last years of chaotic paper folding into worn cornices and cracked fanlights, too much noise was just a rattish sense of forgiveness in the air.

## XI

Why mine this new pace wagging doubt over get over the ash filled song over the clouds as drops of this and that curious quaking to daze our ups and downs drip a favourite tune in strange bathrooms? Empty stands in the street in a beam of ruth stranger than mirrors, relentless green hanging still in the air like a homeless adjective in a notebook on a shelf left bereft by the apparition of a face on the avenue most irrationally. Not benign, not disapproving, just making sure. Still. When the frame is right the rest must keep on inflecting the material calendar here in ninth street espresso on a Monday just between you as you were then even to the original air. Construction all around while coloured bits hang from fences they may even be birds waiting for frills. On home, you could say, iron to forge and swallow as the ground splits and fires burn trees dogs bikes and all, it's a sudden thing to be averted as we wake cut the current to put the day back in.

## XII

Be in the air whoever listens and hug it tight with the grit
needed to find new utility netted on the frame of a photograph. I
was looking for red in deathly grey places, when all was as it was again
in high places, averse to resign from it as currently engaged and
punished for strict laws as more time will take place. Just agreed
to pay this new idea to a blind cause to be linked to net cost
in a mundane record paid off like a collar in fog. You know that red?
And grey? Pebbledash in the mind's eye makes sparse pickings
over wet sand giggling at nothing, down in the mouth and light
at the end of the kettle. Grow up to do that when empty or bolt.
I'm the unconscious slippery legs on time and gossip when
saving breath to keep little else in the fairy tale. Mothers are dead
or would be more so as deals are made by stealth while I may not
sigh in sorrows deep holes in being driven with a wild fear, driven on.

## XIII

The moments of light meant tactile loss enshrined instead from a lost lens by a valued elision in the context itself. They are signal strategies against the flow of history, that's why we're told so. What would you like to represent you, you and your dirty hands say with tears and lamentation? Or is there something as some suppose it is singular. Let me in bed lye dreming of my skin as it hangs from the window ledge whole and deserted, lifted by the October air to frame some view and vow to lose all the coagulated engines of the body. Mint figures mending walls by the last bees seen in the respite frame as if money was virtually no object last for a moment all night as we question whether they are part of the book or cover images. Or covert. Keep driving, not there for the taking an interest or just taking over all the dead that weigh like a night light on the brain which is ever new but groping in the underneath of language for the old translation of things.

## XIV

In the end the flame wherwith I burne consumes the soft
machine itself without breathing; a marble shadow of half-uttered
thoughts, the words gleam against the wall like a laconic
task as all the faces watch and mumble. Laid on plain in careless
new devices as if a select legacy was being played out on
a fiddle inside my skin, its name was broken in the name of some
future form of words, striding forwards to face it until well into
the latent coastlines, the map effaced and stressed and in that sense
being this whole veil reinstated from a single point. Dismantled frontiers
for when things cease to exist or migrate to remain in terror and out
of place. The gift of a tidy world far too loose to imagine or copy
again with the air of a large part of such life, the space of dread inclined
shadowed ignored and rejected in the heart of government. So listen
as my hart dothe seize upon ongoing marks in hand and circumstance for now.

# COLLABORATIVE POEMS

Written with Martin Thom and Nick Totton

# MORE FOLLOWS

[Collaboration with Martin Thom & Nick Totton]

*Cambridge*, 1977

---

*"What on earth are we to do," he said, "with so much beauty?"*
— Hugh Sykes Davies, *Petron*

## *More Follows*

The grammar of living
fingering your larynx (words
like thumbs printing the
air - they kept coming
into my head but
weren't sensational, as usual
I'm sorry, I have
no language I will
not gladly surrender I
have bad news, wake
up this suit is
made to measure dream
dream that's no help
at all literally that's
what I'm worried about.
the window was still
alive my head was
gone, everyone I met
walked off with it
I could see upward
it seemed if you
call that a coincidence
who brings a bandage
for our wounded mouths?
and collects teeth from
the carpet who comes
like breath to the
mouth of the flute?
and replenishes the cupboard
of dreams who suffers?
and experiences repeated bafflement

between now and then
but lives in the
present and will not
gladly surrender.

## *Syringe Song*

day after day we lose
our mutual thought
into "a certain kind of corrupt space"
looking for clues until some strongly felt
residue flares when poked, revives
a hint
of touch. *but will not* by a heartfelt twist
or thumping distortion bring us out to
where we are, our own palindromic
flow, the werewolf at the door you never
jump into twice.
smoke thick above the clock —
can I draw your attention to
carpets under carpets
where puns lurk
the tunnelings of hurt. the habits
of the unquiet mind like those inevitable
things planes do, accompanying
a journey so exhausting the goal
becomes *rest* or it's a question
of ear surgery isn't it but don't
let that put you off; watch all the human
beings go by in their rough colours, their vehicles
their incurable attractions and repulsions
to the terrible journey, their desire
to circle at night like moths with teeth,
for new holes appearing in the banks
of carpets like a tunnel through the wax
that lines the ear.

## *Big Boys Don't Fly*

*Notting Hill carnival, August 1976*

every apparent machine wheeled in
refuses to laugh, lurching out of doors to
        give thanks for the fetish
        the spitting plug in the circuit
        its remaindered blue light
the panic that didn't buy its colour, everyone knows.
        & by what encircles it we "return"
        via monstrous words in the corridor
to the high times proclaimed by the voice
a little ahead of your mouth or so I've heard
        so I've heard, which has been won
        by creation of the earth in carnival green
        by flying machines grounded as gas bleeds
to the last red flecks, there are acres of it,
    the undamaged land offering to the
    damaged the purely private rays
of the moral pair: the man running in the rain
and the life he carries. he states "at this time
        sensation was lost or lessened
        in the limb, and that paralysis
        of motion came on" like daddy
in the guts; but "uneasy" is a tremor in the throat
    of the whole crowd, the police
    are gathering like victims at
the water-hole,
the shift of feet.

## *Taking the Stitches Out*

First, get rid of the atmospherics
and come down to earth through copper wire
into the mind's pocket with nothing to provide
for. It's a slightly omnivorous universe
that picks its teeth carefully while the reserves
build up; the *x* in our sex runs amok
without local anaesthetics, troubling us
for the price of tea and coffee. Each cloudy tax
lights up the skyline, rain melts the world
before it was ready for us and every organ
is refreshed. Quenched wholly, and then
rediscovered through due reflection
in the Chancellor's triumphant smile: he has
balanced it again and we are clawed back
by the love of a good human, all the measures
employed and my stomach turns over
to you, unfulfilled and aching under the button,
no falling star for all those rainy days
when you thought it was you in the glass.

# *Remember Dorking and Damn Malthus*

Playing doctors behind the school we develop
a sense of reproduction, assenting
to the personal pronoun not
through conviction but to cover it up:
making a name for each other till
the syntax jumps for joy on the skyline
minding our dirty business, a giant
leaning towards us like the Menace
of population against which the heads of state pull out
every stop of *vice, misery and self-restraint.*
It's the one way mirror
that cuts us off
in our prime; but sterility
is a scalpel that slices
both ways, and soars on stronger
and stronger towards exposure.
Look into the pram –
the powers that be are right and can
prove it,
there are too many of us and
not enough of them; every bed
in the ward occupied
by rebel forces. Doing it standing up
is no solution, but we can't take it
lying down; we *are* the
future generation, whose *aggregate*
*mass of happiness* collapses into that
large space between tenderness and passion:
a full display exposed, in which the world
is a multiplied through its reflections.

## *Steam Radio*

It just came apart in my hands, the machine whines
so no requests on this programme please;
          it forms a natural vocabulary
in which you may recognise pieces
of yourself. "superstars" is pushing it
                    a bit, pushing it in fact into
                    and through the wall; but where
          do you draw the line is a problem if you've never
          slept deeply, still singing over
the last gurgle of the dirty bathwater, your voice
          a ball that juggles itself
                    on a column of air. you need
          some support? well, don't we all; and meanwhile
          on the tip of your tongue
          blood spurts; a tourniquet
applied to the neck solves several problems
at once, and takes us on into an upbeat
          ending.

# *A Little Stranger*

And he fails to notice the sudden tendency to knit
it together, broken bones and all, into a sentence
that gropes for its predicate and whose general sense
is combustion. There's honey in the old lion
    yet, dreams of vengeance,
        drawn out with sharp instruments
into the main sequence; they must clean up every bit
  of it, and everyone clapped
  the surgical intervention, fat banners streaming
across the wrong strata. "Don't let the air touch
our love, that reaction is quick and final" she cried
    out from the interior he would not
        believe in; and the electrified man
    tried to read more into the same old sky
  a projection of his powers
or his wishes, met by the muzzle and the whip,
by an apparent being
  whose devotees in a frenzy cut off their own
    shadows. Because "she" is him;
   "he" is it; the thumb pushed
through the screen hardly detracts from the illusion,
  like a section through their tissues stained
    cochineal blue
    and refrigerated in sleep. In a
conservative pair they awaited the ikon child.

## *There Is No Parliamentary Road to Happiness*

All right, stuff the present back up the chimney
            sweet animal at hand
no special bodies    of armed men
are going to stop me ascending

Childhoods change hands as seed of the Sun-God, so
they shall never regret, these years!
It's late, capitalism… what merchant ships have my tears?
The voice is chewing the wad, the brain-leaf even now
as light speeds on to enter branded kittens
that march on human breasts incessantly

Enthusiastic doubt falling upwards
step by step, I'll not fade
playing doctors behind a mask of… water?
black milk, phantom regicide
There is so much law
            I can hardly remember the steps

Loyalty to the pronoun, I'm falling down
Loyalty to the syntax, I'm coming back
I trod the mycelium under and over
all I have accumulated is web residue

I'm leaping cracked stones at half-
light until the magic works
and the body cries wolf for good on the stairwell
on each separate occasion I can hardly guess
when the death will happen

I did not marry anything but the writing
Rhythm I took you for my very name
There is so much floating wool
and tooth coat of chalk
my nail and pour half-moon
my private number three at a time
is the ascendant sucking
machine to which the signs defer

## *A Little Too Much Salt*

It doesn't mean a thing, make your move
anyway – lace your boots and hit the tarmac,
we'll talk it over when you come back
in a new plaster cast. Everyone went
home. To assume the dark they smoke how
they make earth fall! The ghost that goes freely
in a mouthful of type awards names
in homoeopathic doses; lie still while saints
like lampreys rise a blue soapy
twist, chanting the soft message
of our dearest and closest to animals. These
relentless visuals are come to deny us
where it hurts: a sweet vision but
unproductive, it completely fills the fire
that smokes us out into the open question
where our deepest disturbance
spells the private number which dissolves
and saturates every solution. A crystal would
set us to rights, its many facets
gleaming and lovely in the midnight sun;
it is cut a little every day, sobs and winks
under the rouge... Have you lost the thread
that stitches you together? and fall
apart into the usual competitive
party games; put them all in the soup,
it tastes so bad they *must* understand.

## *A Separate Section on Hegel*

Let me out, I have to take wing at dusk.

## *A New Kind of Washing Machine*

Knowledge spins in the air beyond the
body's windows as the sink
fills up. That hand draws diagrams
on the pavements, the journey starts
to shrink and unravel in
the tent of night
until there's time to dream it in echoes
bouncing back off the facts of the matter and
we hear the motor's occasional soft music.
The rope pays out.
The hand is smooth despite
its labour and fringes a white, blind body
uncouth against
the subtle political light; or glass
meets and sees through
our open eyes. Without clothes
we are younger than machines,
but the air is older and fills
our lungs thickly till we burst
into speech, sweeter and faster
than ever, it flows over our feet
and gives us enough
to hang the wet items
where the blood spurts
in the sun. We are so clean and
forgiven I can't bear it, we have paid for
the entire cycle and must not
open the machine while it spins.

# *A Disturbance on the Acropolis*

Look, something has been asleep
in this arcade of spinal imagery.
We can hear
the electric self padding down corridors
clicking its fierce shears; we can hear
the turned-down mouth. It takes off another leg
and they all cheer. They hang it
in the backs of cars: in buses, teeth
are displayed in the delighted water
of the upper deck. To be torn
apart, and not die: the wish
that flashes through crowds, the needle sticking
at odd intervals, we need no recognition
but our own. The first cut
is the deepest, is pure choice
and passion, its mending is
invisible or quite simply not present
like a second sleep that sets the dust dancing
on the apparatus. I suppose I just looked at her
with that blank treatment
perhaps, burning out the powers
of the imagination –
you are a pregnant with your father's child
and can hold everyone in your arms
while expanded reproduction lasts
and lasts until the true condition leaves
the interior gazing
on the transfer of power, ripe
yield of these timelines. Desire flies
out of the lesion of normal human

irrelevances with news of birth, death and rebirth
    into another sex, the largest telegram
    in the world between its jaws.

# LOVE LAUGHS AT LOCKSMITHS

[Collaboration with Martin Thom & Nick Totton]

*Curiously Strong*, 1979

---

*The jokes*
*Are ghosts*
*The joke*
*Is a ghost*
*How can you love that mortal creature*
*Every time he speaks*
*He makes*
*Mistakes*
*Two for one*
*Three of us vital*
— Jack Spicer

*The essential ars poetica lies in the technique of overcoming the feeling of repulsion in us which is undoubtedly connected with the barriers that rise between each single ego and the others.*
— Sigmund Freud

your eyes are too big for your
            hands
               to cover
your stomach for your
               heart to find a way          to
your head too much for words

## *Behind the line the life lies*

A lovely frame after some days
of looking around the cloth for
signs of a pattern
quietly emerging as separate housing
estates for my man's body.
This is nothing new,
reading is like this, seeing
the uncanny down a sidestreet
a stirrup-pump or hammer and sickle
encircle one eye
and an ideogram become wine bottles
that shimmers on the table
at the door with his hands on the sill
the lining
that hundreds of people are
trying to call back to put an end to
on some spiked wheel or other.

## *Making a statement fit*

we have ways of making you
      say nothing new
cover walls with it
   nowhere left to slash
nothing obvious in mind
         to damage
no permanency
no dotted line
   no intrinsic cash value

## *For Denise Riley*

nothing in my head
unknotting my fingers by the border
I am return of the rhyme
you can
call me Miriam this time
with a vengeance
at the door with a bunch of lovage
at the window to unknot my view
on the march
to midsummer
and the finished product
in the brass.
A key turns
in the marmite jar
like telepathy from
a passing car

I want it to be something
there before I forget
what I was doing with the whipping-top I was doing
with the spirit dipping too
into jars that circle each uncanny day

That circle each uncanny day
I want it to be something
massing around the blade bone and hugging the wheel
for a warm story of hereabouts
what I was doing with the whipping-top I was doing

With the whipping-top I was doing
nothing in common except perhaps
with his chubby hand on the sill of snap-back
you don't play with the keys at all, you just hit the hammer

## *Men! Write Now*

Fill those embarrassing silences with
    further embarrassing silences before you
acquired one. The sand in your eyes
        is a lot like reading, I mean it's buried,
it's very obscure. I'd like none of it in between.
                                        I like the ending.

## *Wheat Stone Bridge*

throw the pot
into the melting bag and come
back for a few nameless minutes
against the light
the measured resistance
of the old man weeding
down the rows
in a casual glance about
to get down to it:
clean the whole thing up, the warp & weft:
a high flyer
at the top of the morning
in a final steep turn through the clover.
this is the picture woven
in a casual glance, clear and again
clearly helpless.

the real break
is the whole trick, to do it
            with style and grace
saying and I quote
it should be all plain sailing
                        from now on

## *An arrow pointing to the top right hand corner*

*'the streets are my canvas and the people my brush'*
— Mayakovsky

A lovely frame for the bad
        taste works        by the glass works
    in the smelly part of town
    fails to enclose where the transmutation is worked
        right into the gravel, the dog for a walk
passing things on the grass, treading carefully
    from hand to hand and nothing in between
        the toes; passed a good hour
for any whipping boy
full of piss and words and pushing
                towards the best.
Nothing in common but
    one word        is enough for any whipping boy
    and if you canvas *these* streets
    may find a brush you can't bargain with
sweeping the blood clean.

## *Out! Out! Out!*

The whirligig, the crowd
        in which
the spirit of the staircase gets completely lost;
    mnemonic parted from its referent,
grows cancerous, becomes a song
            drawn up in marching order
        to sweep someone or other into the
gutter. Which side are you on, and of which
    street?        which nursery rhyme feeds
            your spirit
        lamp,    what home
land
    fails to enclose you?
The sweet cricketer returns the ball
        another hand caught in the jar
we dum-de-dum
we tra-la-la
    we cannot remember the words

# *Just a friendly warning*

don't go down
            to the woods today, where
the nameless
    excites the eye, where the inner ear
bends to the tumblers' click
            and the door swings open:
there are people
    trying not to sleep in there:
sections of the labour forced
            to be tided away:
there are voices     without references
that fall on a poor soil.
            *to survive what one knows*
                        our prescription is that
you must take the strain
or come off it, into the open rain.

## *Martin Webster sucks, Paul Foot is a fairy*

That old song, how does it go? – Backwards.
The arrow is irreversible
swells over the ranks
drives on into a corner where choices
are counted on the fist of one hand.
Father's moustache, that fatal fascination,
sits up to kiss the spirit lamp; fingers
interlock, and is that
a wishbone, or is it a
skeleton key? I want it to be
something there
before I forget what I was doing…
desperate echoes
split by the roar of the crowd;
they sing on
and on
without a scrap of rhythm, they just don't know
where to stop, they have not
the ghost of a key

## *Strange to think he'll soon be sixty*

In an interesting variant
            the freezer
                really packed out he
died of heatstrike
                      and comes around to it
where I is the first stroke of Me as it later became
and I don't care if you burst into flame

## *The best thing is that it speaks about the future, the worst thing is that it speaks about the past*

the spike in the wheel spoke
the first stroke for any
whipping-boy: there is no place for it
except here, well ahead of the story line
where your hair pin bends
at the heat of Mental Energy,
the beard curls in all directions,
too patriarchal to live
offed with a cut-throat edge
reabsorbed into the compost.
*If I had known I would have been a*
spirit of the staircase:
write the answer on your *own* wall,
the Youth in overalls overhaul
the bridges daily, whitewash
their own night-soil
in a spirit of full employment

## *Suitable for thinking at any time*

as you dish them up reflecting
        chickweed by the taps
distribute food in the places between places
        and don't say anything
don't say anything at all composed
        forget the tape
bury the dog deeper

## *Morphologies*

heave it out or bone up
on everyday lies
drops on sugar, coronation menus
a nasty swirl of boiled pomp
handed to us on a plate.
we walk on the dog
and call it profound
the spirit of
what it is that squats
in the space between landowners
and their dogs
the ghosts of a chance:
for this one time only
be honest and they will survive
knocking at the door
at the table
at our hair like moths

wax spills from
the candle
in your shaky hand

the man on the stair
not there again
returning spirit

covering the same ground
in ghost sheet white
as a light, as a comfort

we carry our fear
as a weapon, as a tool
a rhyme, a desperate echo

we treasure it
we measure it
we bury and exhume it

we cover walls with it

# *Love laughs at locksmiths*

Waving her umbrella the
    old lady sinks into the typewriter, our
money is on toilet training, Einstein to nothing
round the final bend. Our money is on
            whitewash,
on the skids; the lines are drawn
    right down the streets, do not type
above this one
    or below that one.
*Are telepathy and sex incompatible?*
Should they live in separate housing estates
            is the smell
intolerable        irresistible        worked
            right into the concrete.

## *Special offer*

You stand there in buttons
and expect me
like a buried life
just in case
out of reach of the children
on the sand
by the prints of a zip
forcing us through our teeth
into thoughts
slashed
greatly reduced
and not to be repeated

# *Index of Poem Titles*

## #

60 Windows 432

## A

A Bit Apart 97
A Bit Part 311
About the Dark 353
Actual Selection 389
A Disturbance on the Acropolis 480
A Film 253
After Breakfast 49
After Pope 181
A Happy New Year 149
A Hasty Dip 411
Air Flitter 397
A Little Stranger 474
A Little Too Much Salt 477
All Mere Use 419
All Our Ends 53
Allowance to Hand 360
An arrow pointing to the top right hand corner 493
An Ear To Cry On 303
A New Kind of Washing Machine 479
Another Subject Incline 414
A Quieter Light 293
A Reading 80
A Separate Section on Hegel 478
As We Run Out of the Wet 13
Avian 252
A World of Love 201

## B


| | |
|---|---|
| Basic White | 184 |
| Bedevilled Terms | 388 |
| Behind the line the life lies | 486 |
| Big Boys Don't Fly | 470 |
| Bound to a Time | 15 |
| Brown Paper | 276 |
| By the Banks of Grim Margin | 313 |


## C


| | |
|---|---|
| Clear Nothing | 380 |
| Coda | 447 |
| Cold Again | 279 |
| Consolidated Uproar | 355 |
| Coppice Fret Verge | 361 |
| Corncrakes | 259 |
| Could Be | 326 |
| Crossing | 314 |
| Crumpled | 263 |


## D


| | |
|---|---|
| Dark Otherwise | 385 |
| Death of Dance | 203 |
| Deep | 254 |
| Defeated Scale | 384 |
| Derry | 170 |
| Doubtless Matter | 386 |
| Drawn Shapes | 260 |
| Drying Out | 119 |


## E


| | |
|---|---|
| Earlier Pocket | 393 |
| Easy to Say | 256 |
| Empty Space | 278 |
| Endless demands | 42 |
| Exceed Frame Time | 399 |

## F

| | |
|---|---|
| Facing Page | 116 |
| Faint Last Abandon | 358 |
| Fatal Congeries | 12 |
| Fire | 258 |
| Flagrant Number | 378 |
| Footsteps | 277 |
| For Denise Riley | 488 |
| For John James | 436 |
| Free Amble | 312 |

## G

| | |
|---|---|
| Get an Ear Test | 400 |
| Gloomy Clamber | 398 |
| Guinea on China | 83 |

## H

| | |
|---|---|
| Happy Endings | 428 |
| Hardihood | 185 |
| Hardly Yippee | 34 |
| Herman, what makes you tick? | 426 |
| High Time | 84 |
| Holding on to a Stranger | 28 |
| Hold the Child Father Sunlight | 157 |
| How Things Are | 239 |
| Hung Out | 292 |

## I

| | |
|---|---|
| Ideal Fingers | 430 |
| I Felt a Hand Grip My Elbow | 40 |
| Image Damage | 275 |
| I'm Not Sure | 418 |
| Implacable Grasp | 373 |
| Imported Raw | 421 |
| Impression Really | 391 |

Infernal Duo 415
Inlaid Reflection 356
In the Train 204
Intro 23
Intuition Rush 359
Iron Letters 439
Irreducible Blue 59
It Had to be You 56
It Was a Long Lane 39

## J

Japan is Sad 16
Just a friendly warning 495
Just Ignore Them 295
Just Thermal Slash 357

## K

Kara Chach 145

## L

Lapsed Step 375
Last Year's Light 248
Late Capital 58
Laugh Like a Piano 183
Least Ground 377
Least Ignorance 379
Leaving No Trace 406
Lemon Sole 417
Less and Less 113
L'Histoire 81
'Life Dreamed Now Life Lived' (David Gascoyne) 169
Light Paper Material 264
Limbo 315
Lino Cut 99
Living Here Now 206
Look at Them 354

| | |
|---|---|
| Look Back | 98 |
| Looking at Henry | 173 |
| Loud Bees | 288 |
| Love laughs at locksmiths | 502 |
| Lullaby | 153 |


## M

| | |
|---|---|
| Making a statement fit | 487 |
| Man | 14 |
| Martin Webster sucks, Paul Foot is a fairy | 496 |
| Men! Write Now | 490 |
| Metaphorically | 36 |
| More Follows | 467 |
| More Measure | 376 |
| Morphologies | 500 |
| Much More Pronounced | 125 |
| Mulch Tumult | 207 |


## N

| | |
|---|---|
| Nearly Stopped | 374 |
| New York | 176 |
| Night Ministry | 152 |
| Night View | 273 |
| No Contact | 106 |
| North | 205 |
| Northern Line | 304 |
| Not an Object | 291 |
| Notes | 19 |
| Nothing Doing | 370 |
| No Tongue | 243 |
| Not Quite Time | 245 |
| No Way | 267 |

# O


| | |
|---|---|
| Of Art | 285 |
| Of Denser Things | 407 |
| Oh Snooty | 177 |
| Oh, To Be in England | 179 |
| Old Details | 305 |
| One | 274 |
| Only Displacement | 404 |
| Orpheus Says | 365 |
| Out of Date | 38 |
| Out! Out! Out! | 494 |
| Overt Ruffle Return | 362 |


# P


| | |
|---|---|
| Paradise Lost | 286 |
| Pastoral | 180 |
| Past Taste | 405 |
| Peculiar Pertinence | 371 |
| Peep Contact | 392 |
| Pencil | 11 |
| Planted Presence | 372 |
| Please Call Us | 402 |
| Plenty of Nothing | 299 |
| Poem | 143 |
| Poem for Numbers | 437 |
| Politics | 151 |
| Polly Fortune | 155 |
| Postcards to Spain 1986 | 75 |
| Postcard to Italy | 79 |
| Potentially Permanent | 401 |
| pourquoi chercher le bout de la chaîne [...] | 427 |
| Prattle | 61 |
| Protected Wood | 290 |
| Provoke Better | 383 |
| P.S. | 232 |

# Q


Quiet Arriving 147
Quite Right 200


# R


Radish Nostalgia 416
Rebuke 280
Red 257
Red Breath 156
Remember Dorking and Damn Malthus 472
Requiem for a Brain 18
Ritual Slips 154


# S


Saturday 287
Saving Time 325
Say Nothing 93
Seedy Box 271
Sense According 394
Sentinel 17
Sestina 174
Simply That 249
Sleep 102
Small Change 294
Small Changes 82
Solo 88
Some Constants 425
Something in the Air 368
Some Title 123
So to Speak 47
Sparkling Fruit Salts 158
Speaking of Life 60
Special offer 503
Steam Radio 473
Still life 54

Still Visible 246
Strange to think he'll soon be sixty 497
Strong Original 387
Suitable for thinking at any time 499
Summing It Up One of These Days 148
Sunk in the Night 302
Syringe Song 469

## T

Taking the Stitches Out 471
Talkin' Bout Things 24
Tatlin's Dream 33
The Audience 168
The best thing is that it speaks about the future, [...] 498
The Chronicler 43
The Elegy for Spring 144
The Field 283
The First Intervention 86
The Garden Party 100
The light determines a state of absolute rest? 37
The Mode That Will Not Be Written 269
The Name of Day 92
The Night The 73
The Origins of Love and Hate 57
The Political Economy of Art 171
The Progress 329
There Is No Parliamentary Road to Happiness 475
The Scar 327
These Days 109
The Wire 111
The Works 319
The Yurt: Day One 163
Things Reply 25
This and That 104
'This Umber Sea About Us' 250
Tight Orbits 381

| | |
|---|---|
| Time How Short | 63 |
| Title Disputed | 235 |
| Trace | 261 |
| True Rendition | 309 |


## U


| | |
|---|---|
| Uncle Apprehension | 26 |
| Underground | 172 |


## W


| | |
|---|---|
| Waking Up: 2.10 pm | 150 |
| Warning Ignored | 268 |
| We Must Tighten Our Belts | 35 |
| What Ever Next? | 412 |
| Wheat Stone Bridge | 491 |
| When It Seemed That All Was Lost | 87 |
| Where's the Fun? | 289 |
| Wherever a Head | 90 |
| Whirled Attention | 390 |
| Why Call it Again? | 403 |
| Why Motoring Costs Have Soared | 27 |
| Wilding Paper | 420 |
| Will Do | 307 |
| Without Rhyme or Reason | 55 |
| Wood | 241 |
| Wyatt's Voices | 448 |


## Y


| | |
|---|---|
| You Never Said | 62 |

# *Acknowledgements*

These poems cover a period of some fifty-five years during which time I have accrued debts of gratitude to many people, too many to list them all here. What follows is an alphabetical list of those, living and dead, who have been kind enough to publish poems of mine in magazines with varying degrees of ephemerality, or in book or pamphlet form. The generous network of little magazines, online magazines, broadsheets, and independent publishers is an essential feature of poetry cultures and deserves a round of applause. My thanks, therefore, first to Aaron Kent for his care and enthusiasm in putting together this volume; and to Peter Ackroyd, Anthony Barnett, Andrea Brady, Ian Brinton, Fred Buck, Paul Buck, David Chaloner, Andrew Crozier, Philip Crozier, Philip Davis, Taylor Davis-Van Atta, Nate Dorward, Allen Fisher, Paul Green, Chris Hamilton-Emery, Lee Harwood, Ian Heames, Alex Houen, Jane Hughes, Peter Hughes, John James, Boris Jardine, Justin Katko, Aaron Kent, Laura Kilbride, John Kinsella, Andrew Lawson, Tim Longville, Tony Lopez, Barry MacSweeney, Brian Marley, D.S. Marriott, Daniel Medin, Anthony Mellors, Rod Mengham, Drew Milne, Peter Minter, Julia Mishkin, Wendy Mulford, Philip O'Connor, Douglas Oliver, Lara Pawson, Peter Philpott, Adam Piette, Richard Porter, Jacques Rancourt, Tom Raworth, Peter Riley, Luke Roberts, Peter Robinson, Stephen Rodefer, David Rosenberg, Michael Schmidt, Aidan Semmens, Lucy Sheerman, William Sieghart, Iain Sinclair, Simon Smith, Pierre-Yves Soucy, Keston Sutherland, Martin Thom, Nick Totton, John Tranter, John Welch, Neil Wenborn, Nigel Wheale, Lydia Wilson, Mary-Kay Wilmers. My sincere apologies to everyone I've omitted. 'The Plenty of Nothing', first published in *PN Review*, won the 2017 Forward Prize for best single poem.

# LAY OUT YOUR UNREST

www.ingramcontent.com/pod-product-compliance
Lightning Source LLC
Chambersburg PA
CBHW020826160426
43192CB00007B/539
* 9 7 8 1 9 1 5 7 6 0 5 7 9 *